£35

"Picturesque Architecture in Paris,
Ghent, Antwerp, Rouen, etc.
Drawn from Nature on Stone
by Thomas Shotter Boys, 1839"

"Picturesque Architecture in Paris, Ghent, Antwerp, Rouen, etc.
Drawn from Nature on Stone
by Thomas Shotter Boys, 1839"

A Re-issue of the Complete Set of these
Exceedingly Scarce and Beautiful Delineations
of Continental Cities, printed in Colours,
with Descriptive Notes to each Plate, and an
Introduction by

E. BERESFORD CHANCELLOR
M.A. (Oxon), F.S.A.

LONDON
THE ARCHITECTURAL PRESS
9 Queen Anne's Gate, Westminster, S.W. 1
1928

PRINTED IN GREAT BRITAIN FOR
THE ARCHITECTURAL PRESS, LTD.,
BY BILLING AND SONS, LTD., THE
LONDON PRINTING WORKS, GUILDFORD

Boys's Original Dedication.

To

C. Hullmandel, Esq.,

in acknowledgment of

his many great Improvements

and

highly important Discoveries

in

Lithography

this Work

forming another epoch

and

presenting entirely new capabilities of the Arts

is Dedicated by

his sincere Friend

Thomas Shotter Boys

List of Subscribers.

Akademiska Bokhandeln, Helsingfors, Finland.

Messrs. Angus and Robertson, Ltd., Booksellers, Sydney.

The Architectural Association, London, W.C.

The A.S.P. Book Club (*per* J. E. Newberry, Esq.), London, S.W.

James Bain, Bookseller, London, W.C.

Messrs. B. T. Batsford, Ltd., Booksellers, London, W.

Harry Batsford, Esq., Hon. A.R.I.B.A., London.

Messrs. H. K. Beazley and Co., Booksellers, London, S.W.

H. R. Beeton, Esq., Reading.

Public Library, Belfast.

La Bibliothèque Royale de Belgique, Bruxelles.

Messrs. Bickers and Son, Ltd., Booksellers, London, S.W.

Messrs. Biddles, Ltd., Booksellers, Guildford.

Colonel C. F. Birney, Bulawayo, South Africa.

F. E. Bliss, Esq., Santa Barbara, California.

H. Boddington, Esq., M.A., A.R.I.B.A., London, W.

G. Boddy, Bookseller, Middlesbrough.

Darcy Braddell, Esq., F.R.I.B.A., London, W.

Mrs. N. S. Braden, Ontario.

School of Art, Bradford.

Messrs. Brentano's, Inc., Publishers, Chicago, U.S.A.

Messrs. Brentano's, Publishers, Paris.

Messrs. Bright's Stores, Ltd., Booksellers, Bournemouth.

Messrs. G. Broes Van Dort Co., Booksellers, Chicago, U.S.A.

Messrs. Brough and Son, Booksellers, Leamington.

John Brown, Esq., C.B.E., D.S.O., A.R.I.B.A., Northampton.

Messrs. John and Edward Bumpus, Ltd., Booksellers, London, W.

R. M. Butler, Esq., M.R.I.A., F.R.I.B.A., Dublin.

Central Library, Cardiff (*per* Harry Farr, Esq., Librarian).

Carnegie Library, Pittsburg, Pa.

J. P. Chaplin, Esq., Scarborough.

Messrs. L. Chaundy, Ltd., Booksellers, London, W.

Chelsea Arts Club, London, S.W.

Chelsea Publishing Co., London, S.W.

Stephen H. Clarke, Esq., Middlesbrough.

J. G. Commin, Bookseller, Exeter.

La Construction Moderne, Paris.

Messrs. Cornish Bros., Ltd., Booksellers, Manchester.

Frank Crisp, Esq., London, W.

Arthur J. Davis, Esq., F.R.I.B.A., London, W.

Messrs. Dawson's Book Shop, Booksellers, California, U.S.A.

Messrs. Deighton Bell and Co., Ltd., Booksellers, Cambridge.

Solomon M. Delevie, Esq., New York, U.S.A.

Professor A. C. Dickie, M.A., F.S.A., A.R.I.B.A., Manchester.

Messieurs Dietrich et Cie, Booksellers, Bruxelles.

Messrs. Aitken Dott and Son, Booksellers, Edinburgh.

Messrs. T. Eaton and Co., Booksellers, London, E.C.

Cecil G. W. Eve, Esq., B.A., A.R.I.B.A., London, W.

A. C. Fare, Esq., L.R.I.B.A., Bath.
Hedley Fitton, Esq., R.E.
The Fitzwilliam Museum, Cambridge.
Messrs. W. and G. Foyle, Ltd., Booksellers, London, W.C.

The Galignani Library, Booksellers, Paris.
Messrs. Galloway and Porter, Booksellers, Cambridge.
C. P. Garrard, Esq., A.R.I.B.A., Ipswich.
Owen A. J. Goddard, Esq., Finchampstead.
Percy F. Godenrath, Printseller, Ottawa.
Walter H. Godfrey, Esq., F.S.A., F.R.I.B.A., London, S.W.
Messrs. Arthur Greatorex, Ltd., Booksellers, London, W.
Messrs. Gregory's Book Store, Bath.
Frederick J. Gurney, Esq., London, S.E.

Herbert A. Hambling, Esq., London, S.W.
Messrs. Harrods, Ltd., Book Department, London, S.W.
Ernest Hartland, Esq., Chepstow.
J. D. M. Harvey, Esq., London, S.E.
E. Hector, Bookseller, Birmingham.
Messrs. W. Heffer and Sons, Ltd., Booksellers, Cambridge.
F. R. Hockliffe, Bookseller, Bedford.
Charles Hodgdon, Illinois, U.S.A.
Messrs. Hugh Hopkins, Booksellers, Glasgow.
Hugh Hopkins, Esq., Glasgow.

Basil Ionides, Esq., London, W.

Messrs. Jarrold and Sons, Booksellers, Norwich.
E. Peter Jones, Esq., Chester.
C. Sidney Jones, Esq.

Messrs. John Keppie and Henderson, Glasgow.
Carl Wendelin Kuehny, Bookseller, Cleveland, U.S.A.

Messrs. Lamley and Co., Booksellers, London, S.W.
Reference Library, Liverpool.
Libres d'Art (Luis Pou), Barcelona.
London County Council, County Hall, S.E.

J. W. Mackail, Esq.
Walter Makin, Esq., London, E.C.
Reference Library, Manchester.
G. Jervis Manton, Bookseller, Melbourne.
The Medici Society, Ltd., London, W.
Mrs. Medlicott, Newbury.
Metro Goldwyn Mayer Studios, California, U.S.A.
Messrs. James Miles, Booksellers, Leeds.
R. B. Moore, Esq., Ryde, Isle of Wight.
Mowbray and Co., Ltd., Booksellers, London, W.
Messrs. Wm. Mullan and Sons, Booksellers, Belfast.

Public Library, Newcastle-on-Tyne.

Messrs. Palmer, Howe and Co., Booksellers, Manchester.
Messrs. Parker and Son, Ltd., Booksellers, Oxford.
Messrs. Geo. Polley and Co., Booksellers, Boston, U.S.A.
William C. Porte, Esq., M.I.A., Belfast.
Henry I. Potter, Esq., Sheffield.
H. Fellowes Prynne, Esq., India.

Messrs. Bernard Quaritch, Ltd., Booksellers, London, W.

Messrs. Ramsden Bros., Booksellers, Worthing.

List of Subscribers

G. RAPILLY, Librairie, Paris.

MESSRS. HUGH REES, LTD., Booksellers, London, W.

DE REPRODUCTIE COMPAGNIE, Rotterdam. London, S.W.

MESSRS. J. RIMELL AND SON, Booksellers, London, S.W.

MESSRS. RITCHIE BROS., Booksellers, London, E.C.

ROYAL INSTITUTE OF BRITISH ARCHITECTS (*per* Rudolf Dircks, Esq., Librarian), London, W.

RYERSON LIBRARY, Chicago, U.S.A.

MESSRS. CHAS. J. SAWYER, LTD. (Fine Art Department), London, W.

MESSRS. SELFRIDGE AND CO., LTD., London, W.

MESSRS. SHERRATT AND HUGHES, Booksellers, Manchester.

SHOREDITCH CENTRAL LIBRARY (*per* Thos. Green, Esq., Boro' Librarian), London, N.

MESSRS. SIFTON, PRAED AND CO., LTD., Booksellers, London, S.W.

MESSRS. SIMPKIN, MARSHALL, HAMILTON, KENT AND CO., LTD., Booksellers, London, E.C.

SIR JOHN W. SIMPSON, K.B.E., P.P.R.I.B.A., London, W.C.

MESSRS. SIMPSON AND DICKENS, Booksellers, Manchester.

SLOANE BOOKSHOP, London, S.W.

MESSRS. W. H. SMITH AND SON, Booksellers, Cheltenham.

MESSRS. W. H. SMITH AND SON, Booksellers, London, W.C.

MESSRS. W. H. SMITH AND SONS, Booksellers, Newbury.

MESSRS. W. H. SMITH AND SON, Booksellers, Paris.

W. HANNEFORD SMITH, ESQ., F.R.S. (Edin.), Gravesend.

FRANK M. SNYDER, ESQ., New York, U.S.A.

MESSRS. HENRY SOTHERAN AND CO., Booksellers, London, W.C.

MESSRS. G. E. STECHERT AND CO., Booksellers, London, W.C.

PROFESSOR J. E. A. STEGGALL, M.A., F.R.S.E., J.P., Dundee.

MESSRS. B. F. STEVENS AND BROWN, LTD., Booksellers, London, W.C.

LT.-COL. H. H. SUTHERLAND, D.S.O.

MESSRS. D. B. TARAPOREVALA, SONS AND CO., Booksellers, Bombay.

CHARLES E. THOMAS, Bookseller, Worthing.

W. R. THOMAS, ESQ.

THE TIMES BOOK CO., LTD., Booksellers, London, W.

MESSRS. J. TIRANTI AND CO., Publishers, London, W.

MESSRS. TRUSLOVE AND HANSON, Booksellers, London, W.

DONALD VAN DER BURGH, ESQ.

MESSRS. VICARS BROS., Fine Art Dealers, London, W.

R. WAKE, ESQ., Bridgnorth.

WALKER'S GALLERIES, LTD., London, W.

WALLASEY PUBLIC LIBRARIES (*per* W. Wilson, Esq., Librarian).

WESTMINSTER PUBLIC LIBRARY, London, S.W.

E. WEYHE, Bookseller, New York, U.S.A.

SIR ROBERT WITT, London, W.

WOOLWICH PUBLIC LIBRARIES AND MUSEUM (Central Public Library) (*per* Philip C. Bursill, Esq., F.L.A.), London, S.E.

WILLIAM MAURICE WRIGHT, ESQ., M.A., F.S.A., Lincolnshire.

MESSRS. WRIGHT BROS., Booksellers, Boscombe.

MESSRS. HENRY YOUNG AND SONS, Booksellers, Liverpool.

Foreword.

AS in the case of the *Original Views of London,* to which the present volume forms the natural sequel, these being the only two works which Boys issued, I have confined myself, in the descriptive notes, to dealing with the features of each picture portrayed by the artist, although here and there I have had something to say about other characteristics of the cities in which these landmarks appear.

When the *Picturesque Architecture* was published, the twenty-six coloured lithographic plates were accompanied by a folio sheet of letterpress. Part of this was occupied by a general descriptive note, which is so interesting as indicating the method of chromo-lithography employed, and for other reasons, that it is here reprinted in its entirety. The remainder consists of very short notes, sometimes extending to but a few lines, to each of the pictures. These notes required such amplification that I have thought it best, as before, almost wholly to ignore them; although here and there I have incorporated in my descriptions of the plates some interesting fact which Boys had jotted down.

E. B. C.

London, 1928.

List of Plates.

The Original Publisher's Descriptive Notice of "Picturesque Architecture in Paris, Ghent, Antwerp, Rouen," etc.

THE present Work being unique of its kind, and the process by which it is produced entirely new to the public, some account of the means employed is necessary to a due appreciation of the merits of the Artist, and of the qualities peculiar to these printed Drawings; more especially as the specimens put forth have been mistaken for water-colour drawings, or prints wrought up by the hand of the Colourer in imitation of the originals.

The whole of the Drawings composing this volume are produced entirely by means of Lithography: they are printed with oil-colours, and come from the press precisely as they now appear. It was expressly stipulated by the Publisher that not a touch should be added afterwards, and this injunction has been strictly adhered to. They are Pictures drawn on Stone, and re-produced by printing with Colours: every touch is the work of the Artist, and every impression the product of the press.

This is the first, and, as yet, the only attempt to imitate pictorial effects of Landscape Architecture in Chroma-lithography; and in its application to this class of subjects, it has been carried so far beyond what was required in copying poly-chrome architecture, hieroglyphics, arabesques, etc., that it has become almost a new art. The difference may be thus explained: in mere decorative subjects, the colours are positive and opaque, the tints flat, and the several hues of equal intensity throughout; whereas in these views, the various effects of light and shade, of local colour and general tone, result from transparent and graduated tints. The atmospheric appearance of the skies, giving day-light brightness to the out-door scenes, is the best evidence of the purity and brilliancy of the tints of colour; which, being printed in oil on paper, combine solidity with transparency.

In developing the capabilities of Chroma-lithography, the artist has aimed at difference of style in his manner of treatment, as well as at variety in the aspects of nature. For example, the view of the Abbaye St. Amand, Rouen, is intended to present the appearance of a crayon sketch heightened with colour; that of Ste. Chapelle, Paris, a sepia drawing, with touches of colour; the Fish-Market, Antwerp, a slight sketch in water-colours; St. Laurent, a finished water-colour drawing; the Cour of the Hôtel Cluny, an oil-painting; and thus with others. So, with the natural effects, a bright sunny day is shown in the view of the Tuileries; a golden sunset in that of the Institute of Paris; pale moonlight in

xv

that of St. Etienne, with the Pantheon ; a fall of snow in that of Byloke ; and so on. In some,—the street-views of Paris and Rouen, for example,—the local colouring of objects is made predominant ; while, in others,—as in the Belfry, Ghent,—the pictorial effect prevails.

In choosing his subjects, the Artist has been actuated by a desire to rescue from neglect and oblivion some fine relics of picturesque ancient architecture, known only to the curious ; as well as to present edifices more familiar to the tourist under a new point of view, so as to bring out some peculiar features of their respective character. In treating them, he has aimed at accuracy of detail, and fidelity to the general effect of the view, carefully preserving the characteristics of the locality,—in a word, he has endeavoured to convey the actual truth in the most picturesque manner.

The execution of the Drawings, from first to last, is entirely the work of the Artist, Mr. Thomas Shotter Boys, who has devoted his time and talents, with unwearied assiduity, to the arduous task of putting them on stone in this new style of chroma-lithography. The difficulties he has had to encounter have been many and great ; and he can only be repaid for his trouble and anxiety by the satisfaction of having been the first to encounter them, and to open the path of this beautiful art to his brother-artists. To him and to the printer, Mr. Hullmandel, who rendered his valuable assistance in personally superintending the progress of the Work, the Publisher takes this opportunity of expressing his acknowledgments for services which have produced results beyond what he could possibly have anticipated, and which have conferred such a substantial value on the Work, in the perfecting of which neither pains nor expense have been spared.

Introduction.

THE name of Thomas Shotter Boys, which but a few years since was known only to relatively few people, has today become a household word among that large and ever-increasing public to whom great art and the pictorial annals of London make a common appeal. The republication in 1926 of his exquisite memorials of the streets and outstanding landmarks of the city, reduced in size as these necessarily were, made known to many whose attention had not hitherto been drawn to his work, what an extraordinarily vivid picture Boys has left of the London of the earlier years of Queen Victoria's reign. It showed, too, what a masterly hand had been at work perpetuating not merely the topographical aspects of the capital, but also the dress and no little of the manners and customs of the citizens, as seen in the streets, in that now distant day. At a glance one could compare the aspect of, say, Hyde Park Corner or Ludgate Hill, as it was, with the altered conditions that obtain now ; one could smile at the dresses, so archaic as they seem when judged by our present standards, of those who perambulated the thoroughfares ; at the quaint, almost mediæval character of the vehicles which rumbled over the stone or macadam that has been long since converted into wood ; at the obsolete forms of such things as watering-carts and fire-engines ; at those peripatetic trades which were then carried on in the streets, and whose " cries " had at an earlier day been made famous by the beautiful colour-prints of Wheatley and others. In a word, one was confronted with the daily out-of-door life of the London of just on a century ago, and where the buildings forming the background to this activity remain as they were in Boys's time, the differences in the appearance of the actors and the objects in which they were engaged, seem the more novel and strange from this very fact.

But in these pictures not a few of the structures depicted have long disappeared. Not a single building in the Piccadilly of those days (as shown by Boys) remains ; the purlieus of the Tower have changed out of all recognition ; as we have only too good reason for knowing, Regent Street has totally disappeared ; and, if the Banqueting House in Whitehall remains, it is the only structure in the artist's view of that historic thoroughfare that does ; while his representation of the north side of Pall Mall is, in spite of its acute perspective, probably the best picture extant of what that portion of the street looked like before it submitted to the metamorphosis of rebuilt structures.

The London views have thus a double value and significance : they are records of what has gone, and they are records of what certain existing landmarks looked like under conditions different from those of today. It is often forgotten how large a share environment has in the general effect of some familiar and outstanding building. Were it possible to conceive Buckingham Palace ramparted about on each side by insignificant shops, as the beautiful Northumberland House was, how strange and different would be its effect, not only to the eye, but on the imagination ! How wholly foreign to its original intention does not Temple Bar appear amid its present rural surroundings, compared with what it did when it occupied its old site and divided the busy Strand from busy Fleet Street ! And so the value of Boys's *Original Views of London*, as aids to the realization of an earlier London, a London which has now become, through the course of years alone, historic, is incalculable, for they form an almost complete microcosm of the city of a day which is beginning to take the place of a still earlier one, as at once an artistic *motif* and a topographical and historic document of supreme importance.

Three years before these *Views* appeared, Boys had issued a volume on Paris and other Continental cities. The artist's knowledge of the French capital was an intimate one. As I have written an account of Boys's career and works as an Introduction to the *Original Views of London*, there is no necessity for me here to recapitulate the facts of that career ; but it will be well if I recall the incidents of the artist's sojourn abroad.

It was in 1825 that Boys, then twenty-two years of age, paid his first visit to Paris. At that time the outstanding British artist at work there was that extraordinarily precocious and prolific genius Bonington, who was then just two years Boys's senior. It seems not improbable that the younger man went expressly to Paris to get into touch with the elder, and, indeed, it has been affirmed that he actually became his pupil, among others by Ottley, who in his *Biographical Dictionary of Living Painters*, published in 1866, specifically states the fact. This is, however, denied by William Callow, the well-known landscape painter, with whom Boys was on terms of the closest friendship. Callow, in his diary for the year 1831, writes thus concerning the matter : " Shortly after, I became associated with Thomas Shotter Boys, the clever but eccentric artist, who had recently arrived from Brussels. In later years I have seen it stated that Boys was a pupil of Bonington, but if that had been the case I should certainly have known it. Boys never spoke to me of having other than a mere acquaintanceship with Bonington." Be this as it may, there is no doubt—in fact, the figures in Boys's pictures almost prove it—that he must have been largely influenced by Bonington, and probably had the run of his studio, especially as so well-known a critic as Mr. H. M. Cundall, in his *History of English Water-Colour Painting*, suggests that many of the works attributed to Bonington were actually executed by Boys himself.

After doing much illustrative work in Paris for a number of well-known writers and antiquaries, including Baron Humboldt and Baron Denon,* Boys left

* Denon died in 1825, so Boys must have been working for him during the last year of his life ; probably in connection with his *Monumens des Arts du Dessin*, which did not appear till 1829.

Paris for Brussels in 1830; but the Revolution which broke out in that year drove him back to France; not, however, before he had been able to make drawings in the Belgian capital, in Antwerp and in Ghent, which were to form the basis of his lithographs of those cities comprised in the present volume.

It was on his return to Paris that he first made the acquaintance of Callow, with whom he became soon so intimate as to share a studio with him in the Rue de Bouloy, near the Palais Royal. Callow, referring in his diary to this period of his career, remarks that he and his friend " used to ramble about the ancient part of the *cité* of Paris in search of old buildings to sketch." By the " *cité* of Paris " Callow, of course, refers not to Paris as a whole but to that special portion of the capital which lies on the Isle de la Cité and the Isle St. Louis, as well as in the adjacent parts on the north bank known as the Marais and on the south as the Quartier Latin, where the oldest relics of the mediæval capital lingered. It was at this time, no doubt, that Boys made the sketches and studies which he afterwards worked up into the exquisite lithographs which form Plates 12 to 24 in this book. The mediævalism still existing in such a famous building as the Hotel de Cluny; the stern beauty of the contemporary Hotel de Sens; St. Sévérin, with its remarkable windows and the insistent grotesqueness of its amazing gargoyles; the indescribable charm residing in St. Chapelle, where the spirit of its pious founder seems always to dwell; the marked architectural differences between St. Etienne du Mont and the adjacent Pantheon—the Renaissance and the neo-classic—brought into an unexpected apposition; the charm residing in such thoroughfares as those of the Vieille Rue du Temple and the Rue des Bourdonnois; and the dominance over all these of Notre Dame itself, must have exercised a magnetic mastery on one who was so essentially alive to the influence of the past and so receptive of that of the magic of outstanding architectural expression. And it can well be understood how great was Boys's delight in examining and in perpetuating such things, and how determined his efforts to communicate something of his enthusiasm to the friend by his side.

That friend tells us how often he accompanied him on his voyages of investigation, and how often he was encouraged to make sketches as well. " In fact," he adds, " I learned a great deal of the theory and practice of art from Boys, and it was from him I first acquired my love for making water-colour drawings of picturesque old churches and houses." That several of the Paris views owed something to Callow himself seems indicated by the further statement in his diary that " I made some large sketches from the bridges in Paris for Boys, for which he, knowing my love of reading, paid me in books."

In the Victoria and Albert Museum there are several water-colours by Boys which were probably produced at this time, one of which at least formed the original of a lithograph in the present volume, notably that representing the Pavillon de Flore at the Tuileries. Other water-colours in the same collection, as well as in the British Museum, and at least one in the Reinaecker collection,

3

obviously executed at the same period, were not thus, however, reproduced in lithographic form.*

Boys returned to England about 1834, although, according to some accounts, his departure from Paris did not take place till about three years later. Callow is the authority for the former statement, and he was in the best position to know his friend's movements. What seems probable is that Boys returned subsequently to Paris, and that his final departure occurred in 1837. Two years later he issued his first independent publication—the *Picturesque Architecture in Paris, Ghent, Antwerp, Rouen, etc."*—in a single volume of coloured lithographs. This was published by Messrs. Moon, Boys,† and Graves, in folio. It consists of twenty-six pages of plates, but as in three instances there are two small lithographs on one page, the number of separate pictures amounts to twenty-nine. They are preceded by a dedication to C. Hullmandel, the well-known lithographer and authority on the subject, together with descriptive notes to the pictures similar to, but much shorter than, those supplied by C. Ollier for the subsequently published *London Views,* and preceded by an advertisement dealing with this special development of colour lithography. The volume was issued at six guineas, while an extra two guineas was charged for sets mounted on card.

The publication of this volume caused a veritable sensation, for never before had coloured lithography been used as the medium for such robust and beautiful work as that of Boys. According to the latest authority on the subject, Mr. R. M. Burch,‡ Hullmandel had hitherto not markedly succeeded in this medium, although he had already reproduced the work of Harding by its means. " But," says Mr. Burch, " a better draughtsman than Harding was destined to give him his chance, notably Thomas Shotter Boys, whose series of architectural and other studies are not nearly so well known as they deserve to be. One of the best is *Picturesque Architecture in Paris*, etc."

Colour or chromo-lithography had already been established as an art medium for a number of years when Boys issued the Paris views. Without going fully into the matter, which is outside my province here, I may remind the reader that this process was introduced into England by the inventor of lithography himself, Senefelder, in 1803, and was for a time popularized by Rudolph Ackermann, before he fell back on the aquatint as a more convenient method of expression. It is supposed that the first lithographic publications in which coloured inks were used were the facsimiles of certain illustrations by Durer, which were reproduced by Strixner and Piloty at Munich in 1808, probably under Senefelder's superintendence,§ while one of the more notable examples of litho-

---

* There is a " Paris Street Scene—The House of Admiral Coligny " in the Reinaecker collection.
† This member of the firm was a cousin of the artist.
‡ *Colour and Colour Prints*, by R. M. Burch. Pitman and Co., 1910. See also Mr. Martin Hardie's earlier work on the subject.
§ Burch; see, too, Hullmandel's *Manual of Lithography*, 1824 ; second edition, 1832; and a later edition, 1835.

4

graphic work in several colours to be issued was J. A. Barth's *Pacis Monumentum*, published in 1816.

There has been a certain amount of difference of opinion as to the form in which the *Picturesque Architecture in Paris*, etc., was issued. It has been stated that the plates were originally published uncoloured, as in the case of the *Original Views of London*, and that Boys and his assistants coloured them afterwards. Indeed, at least one authority states that he has seen an uncoloured set. I have always been opposed to this opinion, holding that the Paris Views were only published as coloured lithographs and in no other form. And the "Descriptive Notice" regarding them issued by the publisher with the original volume confirms this. For in that notice the following passage occurs: "The present work being unique of its kind, and the process by which it is produced being entirely new to the public, some account of the means employed was felt necessary. The whole of the drawings comprising this volume are produced entirely by means of lithography; they are published in oil colours, and come from the press precisely as they now appear. It was expressly stipulated that not a touch should be added afterwards, and this injunction has been strictly adhered to. They are pictures drawn on stone and reproduced by *printing in colours*; every touch is the work of the artist, and every impression the product of the press. This is the first and as yet the only attempt to imitate pictorial effects of landscape architecture in chromo-lithography."

This precise and authoritative announcement sets at rest any supposition that the plates were issued uncoloured, especially as it is corroborated on the title-page of the book where, at the bottom of the page below the name of the publisher, it is expressly stated that the work is "printed entirely in colour by C. Hullmandel."

But as there seems no doubt that uncoloured copies have been met with, my conclusion is that as these are admittedly very rare, a few may have been pulled in this state as specimens, or perhaps with the intention, probably not carried out, of putting on the market both plain and coloured sets.

The *Picturesque Architecture in Paris*, etc., was the result of Boys's exquisitely artistic work superimposed, as it were, on Hullmandel's earlier investigations into what was then a novel medium, but one which, for a time, became fashionable, only, however, to degenerate finally into the commonplace when used as the means of advertising new songs and such-like things, until in recent days the rarity of coloured lithographs, especially where they reproduce true artistic work, has caused them to be sought after with an enthusiasm hitherto confined to the collection of eighteenth-century and early nineteenth-century colour prints.

An anecdote is connected with the publication of the *Picturesque Architecture in Paris*, which, although I have given it in the introduction to the *London Views*, may be repeated, as it properly finds a place here. Callow was asked to present a copy of the book to Louis Philippe, and this he did through the

Princess Clementine to whom he was known. The volume was graciously accepted, and not long afterwards the King sent a diamond ring to the publishers as a testimony of his recognition of the beauty and merits of their gift. When Boys heard of this he was greatly annoyed and disappointed, as he not unnaturally thought that he, as the only "begetter" of the work, should have been the recipient of the jewel. Of course, as Callow points out, the mistake occurred through the publishers and not the printer presenting the volume. However, when the *London Views* appeared three years later, Boys himself took care to send a copy to the King, when that monarch presented the artist with a valuable watch, accompanied by a letter sufficiently flattering in tone to obliterate his previous feeling of disappointment.

It is, perhaps, unnecessary here to expatiate on the artistic charm coupled with the architectural and topographical excellence of these lithographs. The reproductions of them, although on a necessarily smaller scale than the originals, afford sufficient proof of this. Notwithstanding that in some ways their subjects are not so generally familiar to us as the well-known outlines of our own capital, these views of Paris and other Continental cities depict spots with which many people are almost as conversant as they are with certain London landmarks. Paris has today become so accessible to us, while Antwerp and Ghent and the other cities here represented are all so relatively near us that many readers will only be less intimate with them than they are with places within our own boundaries, and Americans will be found, perhaps, even more at home in them. Thus these views have the charm (beyond their artistic and topographical attractions) of representing the past aspects of buildings, the majority of which are still known to us. As beautiful pictures alone they possess undeniable merit ; as historical documents they have a further value ; as topographical data they are singularly precious. And they have another claim to attention ; each of them represents an object picturesque in itself. The mediævalism which, unlike the case of London, can still be found in Paris, in spite of the rebuilding and Haussmannizing to which the city has been subjected, lends itself to artistic treatment in a quite definite and peculiar way. The beauty of such churches as St. Sévérin and St. Etienne du Mont ; the old-world *aura* which still pervades such landmarks as the Hotel de Sens and the Hotel de la Trémouille ; the exquisite outlines of Notre Dame and Sainte Chapelle, each affords material for the pencil of the artist and the pen of the topographer in a quite special way, and in a way which through a collocation of circumstances is unfortunately not possible in London. Again, in the case of the views of other French and Belgian cities, the same fact emerges ; while through the baneful results of events too recent to be further explored with equanimity, and never to be forgotten, such places as Antwerp and Arras and Ghent have impressed the minds even of those unfamiliar with them, and thus give these renderings of them, as they were in earlier times, an added interest and significance.

A still further importance may be claimed for these reproductions of Boys's

Continental views taken in conjunction with the former volume, and it is this : that here we get through the medium of one of the greatest masters of artistic *cum* topographical expression a picture of what the two outstanding capitals of Europe looked like at a period just upon a century ago.   We can compare their buildings so far as Boys here delineates them ; we can compare the varied life of their streets, and the differences in the dress of their inhabitants, and so forth. Almost have we here a microcosm of our outward forms of existence as differentiated from that of those who are really so near us, but whom the blue strip of Channel divides so completely.

These two volumes, the only ones which Boys issued, thus form commentaries on each other, and, taking Paris as the dominating feature of the present one, represent " the tale of two cities " as exemplified in their buildings and their streets, and to no little extent in the manners and customs of their inhabitants.

As I append descriptive notes to each of the twenty-nine plates which follow, it is unnecessary for me here to say more than I have done by way of introduction ; but I may, perhaps, be permitted to add the hope that this volume will achieve the popularity which it would be false modesty on my part to pretend that the *London Views* has not secured.   Nor need I say " false modesty," for no one realizes more than I that not what I have done as a showman, so to speak, has caused this result, but the growing and ever-increasing recognition on the part of the public of the consummate achievement of the man whose work was so long generally neglected, but who has at long last come into his own.

7

The Plates

IN this pictorial introduction to Boys's illustrations of old Paris and other Continental cities, the actual representation of an existing landmark is made more or less subsidiary to the letterpress itself. In the *Original Views of London* this was not so much the case, and as Boys selected as a kind of introductory picture to that series a feature of our city which was, and is, among its most memorable landmarks, it only required a portrayal of the chief features of its exterior to satisfy the reader, who would almost certainly be acquainted with the Temple Church thus represented. Here, however, Boys has selected a relic which in the thirties of the nineteenth century existed in a street which even to Parisians cannot have been generally known. Today not only has this delightful little Renaissance doorway disappeared (the building to which it was attached was destroyed in the Revolution of 1792), but the very street which it dignified has long since ceased to exist. You may spend hours over a map of Paris, and you may range Bottin through and through, without discovering a Rue de la Licorne or any trace of it; for it is not even one of those little thoroughfares that have, after a favourite French custom, been renamed. It is as much swept from the face of the city as if it had never been, and its history, if it had any, is with itself wholly lost.

To discover where it was you must have recourse to a very curious plan of Paris executed in tapestry during the sixteenth century on very similar lines to those the Sheldons produced in this country, some of which are in the Victoria and Albert Museum, and one of which Horace Walpole presented to Lady Aylesbury. The French example is in the Bibliothèque Nationale, and by it we shall see that among the mass of buildings and intersecting streets which once occupied the space in front of Notre Dame, a space now dominated more or less by Charlemagne on his warhorse, was the Rue de la Licorne, which ran north and south between the Rue des Marmousets (or, as it is here written, Marmouses, about which I have something to say further on in this volume) and the Rue la Tuifrie, the great buildings of the Hotel Dieu actually standing on the site through which the little thoroughfare ran.

There was never probably a more thorough clearance of old streets and houses in Paris than when the Place du Parvis de Notre Dame, as it is called, was enlarged by gradual processes until, in 1882, the great square emerged as we see it to-day. Even at the time of the Revolution the space in front of the cathedral was exiguous to a degree and was bounded by the ancient Rue St. Christophe, which was within but a few yards of the three west doors of the cathedral. The open space was then in all about a quarter the size of the present one, and in remote times a large number of churches and chapels attached to religious houses and other institutions nestled close to Notre Dame and found security by their proximity to the royal residence near at hand. For in those times this was the centre and as it were the core of the city, and the two chief islands forming this enceinte were to Paris what the City, bounded by its walls and entered by its gates, was to London.

1. *Rue de la Licorne, Paris*

Thus every street in it may be regarded either as among the oldest or at least the direct descendants of the oldest in Paris. But as in course of time the citizens migrated westward in the wake of the court, this old site was left to the undisputed possession of the great cathedral, which towered above its then architecturally low buildings.

If the Rue de la Licorne, therefore, had any notable inhabitants or was the scene of any notable event, the record of them has been lost except in one instance : for it is known that here at one time dwelt that Jean Pitard, surgeon to Louis IX., whose name may be found in the chronicles dealing with that saintly monarch, which date his residence here somewhere about the middle of the thirteenth century, although how long before that the street was built is " wropt in a mistry," as Yellowplush has it.

It would be interesting if it could be proved (but who is to prove it?) that the beautiful relic perpetuated in the terms of his gracious art by Boys was the entrance to the house occupied by Pitard. It would be a pleasanter memory to have than many which haunted this area, where once existed Le Glatigny, or Val d'Amour as it was suggestively called, and the Rue aux Fèves, familiar to readers of Eugene Sue's *Mysteries of Paris* (if anyone is now familiar with that eerie work), or this very Rue de la Licorne itself, where once the famous Cabaret de la Pomme de Pin was situated, immortalized by Rabelais as " parmi les méritoires tavernes hantés par les escoliers de Paris."

One likes to think that this doorway was once a part of a religious house; in fact, the empty niche may well once have contained a saint or the Virgin herself, to whom we may imagine Villon doffing his hat as he passed from inditing a *villanelle* to committing a theft or even a murder, so complicated was the point of view from which such as he regarded life in those spacious days. In any case, wandering across the rather arid area which we now have in place of the houses and streets of those far-off times, we may re-echo once more the poet's haunting refrain :

Où sont les neiges d'antan.

IT is appropriate for two reasons that Boys should have given us, as he does in this picture, a view of Antwerp's Fish Market. In the first place, the city is Belgium's chief seaport on the Scheldt estuary, its very name, as known in Flemish, Antwerpen, signifying " at the wharf "; and, therefore, the fish market may be said to be the characteristic feature of the place. Again, Antwerp's more notable landmarks, the Cathedral, the Hotel de Ville, poor as it is in comparison with such masterpieces as those of Bruges and Brussels, Ghent and Louvain, the Plantin Museum, and so forth, are so generally well known, as indeed they were in the artist's day (for Antwerp was one of those places which have always been specially cosmopolitan), that he naturally sought for something to perpetuate, in terms of art, which was more likely to be overlooked than the more recognized sights.

Thus it happened that Boys has preserved for us here something which in his accompanying note he prophetically surmises " has probably by this time been pulled down." What he gives us is a general view of the market, making the monument in the foreground the *point d'appui* of his composition, as it were, and at the same time being able to flank the low stalls and so forth with a larger building in the background. The grotesque column which forms the main feature of the picture was called Rubens's Pillar, although for what reason has eluded the present writer. However, the name gains an additional significance to Boys's choice of subject, for, as all the world knows, Rubens was an Antwerp man by descent and education, although, as all the world may not remember, he was actually born not here but at Siegen, in Nassau. But Antwerp connotes the career and fame of that amazing and splendid creature, that flamboyant personality, that dashing swashbuckler of the arts. You remember Thackeray's great eulogium of Rubens in his " Notes on a Week's Holiday," and how he closes his famous description by saying, " I can't look at Rubens's pictures without fancying I see that handsome figure swaggering before the canvas." Well, I think, no one can be in Antwerp without mentally visualizing the artist's compelling personality passing along the streets which seem in the imagination filled with the famous flowing lines of his dominant hat—the very personification of graceful self-satisfaction, the hall-mark of artistic perfection. And so whether he had any particular connection with it or not, one can understand the people of Antwerp associating that great name with the column.

The building in the background of the picture was the old town prison, and to use Boys's own words the market-place itself was in his time " a motley assemblage of portraits and statues, saints and cod-fish, ' Our Lady ' and lobsters, the heterogeneous decoration of a pump, or as it is called, a fountain." By which we see that Boys besides being a remarkable artist had also a pretty wit. The point of his remarks is illustrated by the subsidiary features in his picture, which, by the way, is signed and dated 1839.

2. *Hospice des Vieillards, Ghent*

2. *Fish Market, Antwerp*

THE Emperor Charles V., who was born at Ghent, once said that he could put Paris in his *Gant* (Gand), a kind of jest which a generation which loved plays on words no doubt duly appreciated. But curious as it may seem to us today, there is no doubt that Ghent (as we spell it, Gand being, of course, the French form of the word) was in earlier days a place of immense size and far greater importance than it is today, when it connotes rather those beautiful architectural features of a past age than any other special outstanding character in other directions.

Boys has disregarded the more hackneyed features of the city with which the visitor is assumed to be familiar, and has here given us a delightful little rendering of the Hospice des Vieillards, or almshouses for old men, about which even the guide books cannot bring themselves to be eloquent, so occupied are they, and not unnaturally, with the descriptions of the outstanding landmarks of the place—the Cathedral, the Town Hall, and the lesser churches, and in dissertations on their architectural and other attractions. The picture before us almost speaks for itself. But I may note that the basement is early Gothic work, and may draw attention to the beautiful arcades of pointed arches on Norman columns which flank the wooden entrance, itself of relatively modern construction. The perpendicular windows also deserve examination; while in the background the wall is pierced by a doorway giving on to the garden of the Hospice, one of the trees of which is seen rising above the wall, its greenery forming a pleasant contrast to the mass of ancient buildings in the foreground. To give a characteristic touch to the composition Boys has placed the figure of a monk entering the porch. The picture is signed T. Boys, and dated 1839.

ON one occasion Erasmus remarked that there was not a town in all Christendom to compare with Ghent for size, power, political constitutions, or culture. The claim sounds, nowadays, extravagant enough, but in the past there is no doubt that the place did occupy a position of sufficient importance to give some colour to what must, however, in any case have been, to use our charming elegance of speech, a tall order. Nowadays we think of Ghent as one of those mediæval Flemish cities (Bruges is another) in which the beauty of the architectural remains and the fame of its pictorial celebrities have cast into the shade their importance as political and civic centres. That Ghent, however, did formerly impress even those who were accustomed to outstanding splendour is evidenced by an anecdote concerning Charles V. and the Duke of Alva. When the latter ruthless soldier, during his tyrannical overrunning of the Netherlands in 1547, proposed to destroy the city, he was asked by the Emperor to accompany him to the top of the famous Belfry. Arrived there and surveying the city spread out on all sides beneath them, Charles demanded, "Combien faudrait-il de peaux d'Espagne pour faire un Gant de cette grandeur?" the play on the words being a pleasant method of reproving his too sanguinarily-minded general for his dreadful suggestion. It is this Belfry, on which the Emperor and his vicegerent stood three hundred and eighty years ago, that is the subject of Boys's beautiful and spirited picture, and which, with the Cathedral of St. Bavon, forms the most important and interesting feature of Ghent, or Gand, as the French call it and as the artist himself sometimes writes it.

From this cathedral the Rue St. Jean leads directly to the spot where the great tower rises, the gilded dragon of which faces you as you advance. It was designed roughly about the year 1183, and is, therefore, approximately a century older than the Belfry at Bruges, which was not begun till 1291 and completed a century later. But although it had thus been meditated so early, its actual construction was delayed, for one reason or another, to such an extent, that it was not till 1321 that it was actually begun, and even then it occupied eighteen years in building. As may be seen, it is a remarkable specimen of early Gothic, and its immense altitude is thus accounted for by Boys in his descriptive note to his picture : "The great height of these clock towers was in order to allow of sufficient depth for the descent of the weights then used in the machinery of town clocks." It possesses a wonderful "carillon," or peal of bells, which chime the quarters and play a tune at the hours. The chief of the bells is known by the name of Roelandt. The original windows of the tower have been walled up, and the tapering turret which now crowns the tower is unfortunately of modern construction, and of iron at that. On the top stands the large gilded dragon which, according to general tradition, was brought from St. Sophia at Constantinople to Bruges by Baldwin IX., Count of Flanders, when he returned from the fourth Crusade, in 1204, he having assumed the title of Emperor of Constantinople in the previous year. In 1382 the dragon was, however, carried away as a trophy from Bruges by the people of Ghent, under Philip Van Arte-

3. *The Belfry, Ghent*

velde, after the defeat of Louis III., Count of Flanders, on May 3 of that year. So much for the legend to which a certain semblance of probability might possibly be given, having regard to the Oriental character of the monument. But a learned gentleman, delving among the archives, has since produced documentary evidence which seems to show conclusively that the dragon never was, as a matter of fact, either in the capital of Turkey or in the capital of West Flanders at all, but was actually made in Ghent itself, in the year of grace 1380 ! By the way, some years ago, a Méryon-like etching representing the raising of this famous landmark to the top of the Belfry was produced by Jules de Bruycker. The mediæval building seen in the picture on the right of the Belfry, in which, in Boys's time, public auctions were held, is the Cloth Hall, which was erected in 1424, but has been restored at various times. It is of the Decorated Period, and there are a number of niches for statues, all of which are empty. Beneath the Belfry is, by the way, the municipal prison, which goes by the name of Mammelokker, from a bas-relief of a Roman woman suckling her father, intended to excite charitable feelings in the passers-by. It is of the eighteenth century, when they loved to rope in classic tradition for such purposes, but is an anachronism on the building it is supposed to adorn.

The presence of the many small figures introduced by the artist into his picture helps to emphasize the extraordinary height of the tower, which is its chief feature. Although signed by Boys, the lithograph is undated.

THOSE who are acquainted with our old English word Lock as applied to a hospital, a word emanating, of course, from the French *loques* indicating a rag or lint used for wounds, might rush to the conclusion that this picture by Boys represented an establishment of such a character, Byloke being easily associated with lock or *loques*, and that our old Lock Hospital in Grosvenor Place, later moved to Westbourne Green in the Harrow Road, had its more picturesque counterpart in Ghent. The fact is, however, that the word "byloke" merely means " by the lock," the lock in this case having nothing to do with rags or wounds, but being simply one of the divisions of the River Lys at whose junction with the " lazy Scheldt " of Goldsmith's phrase Ghent stands. As a matter of fact, however, this Byloke did, in course of time, by a curious co-incidence, become the principal hospital of the city, and as such Boys, in his short descriptive note to the picture before us, refers to it. So that the supposition of the amateur etymologist would not, in a sense, have been so far out after all.

This hospital, we are told, was one of very considerable size, it having accommodation for no fewer than one thousand patients. The curious thing about it was that its interior was not divided as is usual into a number of wards with beds for a relatively limited number of occupants in each, but was, as it were, cut up into two immense chambers in each of which as many as five hundred beds could be placed. These beds were ranged in triple rows, and one imagines that the sight of them filled with the sick and dying must have been calculated to make the stoutest hearts quail. Happily we are not called upon to do anything but admire the exterior of the building; and of that exterior the artist has naturally selected for perpetuation one of the most attractive features. For nothing can be more charming than the gable filled with its beautiful tracery which here confronts us, a characteristic to be found, of course, in various places in Flanders, but one which is none the less always capable of exciting in us that pleasant feeling which the great Goethe, as a boy, experienced when he contemplated the gilded weathercock at Frankfort.

Close to this Byloke, but beyond the River Lys, the Counts of Flanders erected in early days a strong castle called the Gravenstein or Oudeburg, and this helped to protect the two streams whose junction occurred at this point, and thus gradually attracted merchants and others to settle under its ægis. It was, therefore, natural that such a building as the Byloke should have been placed in a position at once safe and convenient ; especially was this natural when we know that in earlier times the Byloke had been a nunnery or what is called in Belgium a *béguinage* (from one Lambert Bégue, who erected the first of its kind in 1180). Today there is what is called the *Grand Béguinage*, in Ghent. But this is in a different position, being situated on the Antwerp Road ; and instead of being but a single picturesque structure, is little less than a miniature town, enclosed by a moated wall, but otherwise having no special artistic or antiquarian interest.

4. *The Byloke, Ghent*

One could have wished that Boys had given us other views in this pictur-esque city : the Cathedral of St. Bavon, for instance, in which may be seen the font in which Charles V. was baptized, and some candelabra once belonging to our Charles I. ; besides its chapels with pictures by such great Flemish painters as the Van Eycks, Van der Meiren, Crayer, and the rest, or the Maison de Bateliers, facing the Lys, that fine specimen of domestic architecture of the early sixteenth century. But as we see, he has at least selected a picturesque subject, although he has treated it in a way unique for him—I mean by showing it to us in an environment of snow.

There was, however, a reason for this. As is mentioned in the Descriptive Notice (which is reproduced in this volume), he aimed at " difference of style in his manner of treatment, as well as at variety in the aspects of nature," in order to show the capabilities of chromo-lithography, and he specially quotes this " fall of snow in that of the Byloke " as differentiating the composition from the bright sunny day in the view of the Tuileries, the golden sunset in that of the Institute, and the pale moonlight which suffuses that of St. Etienne du Mont, and so forth.

On the whole, however, I am inclined to think this is the least successful of Boys's pictures in his *Picturesque Architecture*. The architectural features are, indeed, excellent, but the prevailing whiteness is rather monotonous, and, incidentally, the cows introduced into the picture are not such animals as one would have liked the artist to give us. The scene suffers, too, in my opinion, from the absence of figures, for if there ever was a painter who was not only amazingly accurate and attractive in his presentation of architectural effects, but who was also a supremely excellent delineator of human beings as they stood or sat or walked about the cities of which he has perpetuated so many beauties, it was Thomas Shotter Boys.

BOYS chose this view partly to show the irregularities of this part of Dieppe, and partly to preserve pictorially a beautiful and interesting feature of the place. Dieppe today is so different from what it was when the artist stayed there and made his drawing of the Tour de Remi in 1839, that were his ghost to revisit the glimpses of the moon it would be hard put to it to find its way about. A great " plage " stretches along the sea-front, and a casino and a bazaar are almost cheek by jowl with the old and picturesque castle with its massive fifteenth-century masonry set up as a defence against the English, which was so terribly knocked about by the bombardment of these same troublesome people from over La Manche in 1694. Dieppe today connotes two things : the first stage on one of the journeys to Paris, or a seaside resort where people go to gambol in the water, or mildly to gamble in the casino, frequently to do both. When Boys was there the place had hardly forgotten its more strenuous past, and no more dreamed of its fashionable apotheosis than did Brighton in the eighteenth century, or Bexhill in the nineteenth.

Dieppe is one of those composite seaside towns, so to call it, which has one hand on trade and the other on amusement, in this respect being not unlike Hastings. Its fishing fleet is famous. It has its docks, the Avant Port and the Nouvel Avant Port, its Bassin Duquesne and its Bassin Bérigny, and the rest ; it has also its promenades and its Casino, and it is behind the latter that the Rue St. Remi runs, close by which stands the Castle with the Church of St. Remi near at hand.

In making his drawing, Boys, I imagine, took up a position at the junction of what were then the Rues de la Grève and de Sygogne, so that he was able not merely to introduce the beautiful relic which the bombardment of 1694 spared, but also to contrive an effective ensemble composed of the old houses in the neighbourhood.

There are only two interesting churches in Dieppe, as the artist himself states in his note to this picture : that of St. Remi and that of St. Jacques, although he does not specify them by name. The former is in the composite style of the sixteenth and seventeenth centuries, and contains extraordinarily large columns, some of which, in the choir, have their capitals elaborately carved. There are some good examples of sculptured work in the Lady Chapel, but otherwise there is not much to detain anyone. The Church of St. Jacques is a far more elaborate structure, standing in the middle of the town, and flanked by the Rues de Mortier, Ste. Catherine, and St. Jacques. It is in the more florid Gothic style, and its earliest portion dates from the twelfth century. Of it Fergusson has remarked " its lace-like beauty of detail and elaborate finish, which charms in spite of soberer reason, that tells us that it is not in stone that such vagaries should be attempted." Perhaps it was for this reason that Boys did not also execute a picture of it while he was in Dieppe, or, if he did, why he thought well not to include it in his *Picturesque Architecture*.

The Tower of St. Remi, of which the artist here gives us so charming a

5. *Tour de Remi, Dieppe*

picture, appears to have been almost the only part, curiously enough, of that church which was not damaged by William III.'s pin-prick at his hated rival, Louis XIV. The structure had only been completed a little time before the bombardment, and, among other things, the roof of the choir was totally destroyed. With regard to the Tower itself, Boys remarks that " it is evidently not carried to its proper height, and the roof is not in character with its architecture."

Examining the picture before us we shall see that, as usual, certain figures, nine in all, are introduced in order to give life and movement, and as a foil to the inanimate interest residing in old stones. The two men carrying luggage on a hand-barrow indicate the position of Dieppe as a port ; the beggar asking alms from a passer-by, a Daumier sort of man, is a characteristic touch not peculiar to Dieppe. The mounted horseman, the boy filling a pitcher from a conduit, and the soldier standing at attention, all help to fill the foreground, while the man on the top of the steps carries one's eye from these figures up to the pink and delicate tower which is the chief object in the composition. The old houses in the foreground complete the picture, which those who know Dieppe as it is now should find rather intriguing.

I have searched for a signature and date, but can find neither. In fact, the "Bière et Cidre" on the house in the left foreground, with the initials A. G. above (whatever they may stand for), is all the writing which Boys, who generally liked to put such matter in his pictures, here vouchsafes us.

THE word "Arras" connotes two things : one, the famous town in what used to be called the French Netherlands, and the other those wall-hangings first manufactured there, of which we hear so much in old records and of which Shakespeare makes such dramatic use in *Hamlet* and *King John*, besides giving them a comic significance in connection with Falstaff.

Here, of course, we are only concerned with the town itself, and more particularly with that famous Town Hall which suffered so terribly during the Great War. It is, indeed, in consequence of these later sinister events that Arras has become known to many who might not otherwise have been acquainted with it, and by name, at least, to thousands who never before knew of its existence.

Before saying anything about the lovely feature which was the *raison d'être* of Boys's picture, I may properly take the opportunity of saying a word here concerning the place itself and its past history. That history goes back to Roman days when, as the chief town of the Atrebates, Arras was known as Nemetacum. Even so early as the fourth century the place was notable as an important centre for the manufacture of woollen materials, for whose dyeing the madder which grew abundantly in the neighbourhood formed an excellent medium. But it was during the Middle Ages that its wall-hangings became famous throughout Europe, being in course of time generally referred to as " arras."

In the days when this part of Europe was in a state of flux and continual turmoil, Arras found itself now dominated by France, anon by Burgundy, again by Germany and Spain. Indeed, it had experience of so many different masters that it must have been difficult for it, under such constantly changing conditions, to realize to whom it owed allegiance. From these domestic experiences (so to term them) the town emerges into more prominent history as the place where the treaty of peace between the English and the French was signed after the Battle of Agincourt. During subsequent struggles between France and her neighbours, Arras again changed hands according to the varying fortunes of the combatants ; but in those days it would seem that it preferred the governance of any rather than that of the French, for it is known that when Louis XI. became definite master of it by the Peace of Arras in 1482 he changed its name to Franchise, a name, however, which, in spite of royal mandate, did not stick, probably owing to the death of the monarch in the following year. It was not, indeed, till 1659 that Arras became irrevocably incorporated with France, which country had made itself master of it in 1640, but only held it, so to speak, on sufferance, the Spaniards desperately attempting to regain it in 1654. It has since those days been so incontestably French that one has some difficulty in visualizing it as having owed allegiance to any other Power.

Amid the picturesque beauties of the place, its churches and its old houses, its modern Tour des Ursulines (built in imitation of an earlier one), and its glorious Hotel de Ville, the sad fact emerges that Arras was the birthplace of at

6. *L'Hotel de Ville, Arras*

least three men who became more or less notorious during the French Revolution. Of these the most important was the "sea-green incorruptible" of Carlyle's famous and unforgettable phrase. Maximilien Robespierre was born here on May 6, 1758, and here practised as a lawyer before fate carried him into the larger world, and, on July 28, 1794, to the guillotine, to which he had sent so many innocent people. His younger brother, Augustin Joseph, who was executed on the same day, was also born in Arras ; and Joseph Lebon, once a *curé*, who lived to be the organizer of the Terror in Arras itself, was also a native of the place. One imagines that the town is not specially anxious to remember its triumvirate of infamous men.

It is quite time to turn from these details to the beautiful picture before us. In it Boys has given us one of the most attractive of the many delightful representations which art has consecrated to the perpetuation of this lovely landmark —the famous Hotel de Ville. That fabric is one of the most exquisite examples of the Gothic convention as applied to such public buildings. No record of the actual structure or the date of its erection is known to exist ; but it was probably constructed during the latter part of the fifteenth, or beginning of the sixteenth, century, although here and there the purist will detect the deteriorating effect of the mixture of later classic details. Boys draws particular attention, in his note to this picture, to the bizarre character of the crown which forms so striking a finial to the tower. He also takes occasion to make, like President Hénault, a philosophical observation concerning the cupolas which dominate the buildings of this part of Europe. "It is remarkable," he writes, "that, as the traveller approaches the Netherlands, the little cupolas or bulbous terminations of the spires gradually assume a more taper form, verging from the melon to the pear shape."

The care with which the artist has copied every detail of the exquisite façade of Arras's Town Hall precludes the necessity of writing a descriptive account of its architectural features. The architect will know and realize these; the plain man will rather delight in the general *ensemble* of beauty which it affords. Both, however, should not overlook the delicacy and charm of the structure to the left of the Hotel de Ville, to which it is worth drawing attention, as otherwise a contemplation of its wonderful neighbour might cause it to be ignored.

LAON, except by name to railway travellers, is not, I think, a very well-known place. I confess that although I have passed through it, and on one unforgettable occasion had to wait a couple of hours in the dead of night at its station, I am not acquainted with it except in the most cursory way, and I have therefore to fall back on what I can find written by those luckier than myself, in the way of descriptive narrative, and on the beautiful picture of a portion of the famous cathedral which Boys here presents to us.

Although Laon has, today, fallen from its high estate, it was once the home of kings, the later Carlovingians making it their favourite place of residence; and even long before then it had been an important Roman settlement under the varied names of Bibrax, Laudunum, and Lugdunum Clavatum.

During the Middle Ages it seems to have chiefly occupied itself by asserting or trying to assert its independence against certain great Churchmen, its Bishops, who were constantly assailing the liberties of its citizens. Later it became linked on to our own military history by being occupied by the English for just on twenty years from 1410; while during the struggle connected with the League, formed in 1576 to support the Roman Catholic interest, it was the scene of much turbulence—the religious differences of those times always seeming to have found a special centre for displaying themselves in this part of the country. It was, to come down the centuries, under the walls of Laon that Blücher defeated Napoleon, in 1814, a deed of military prowess matched when, in 1870, the Germans entered the town with little or no opposition except from one devoted citizen named Henriot (his name deserves recording), who blew up the powder magazine as the enemy was entering the citadel and killed himself, as well as far more Frenchmen than Germans, in the act.

There are here, as in nearly every French town, a number of interesting landmarks: the Museum; the fine Library; the Hotel de Ville, with its "Place" in which stands a statue of Marshal Sérurier who was born here; its Palais de Justice, formerly the Bishop's palace, dating from the thirteenth century, and its church, dedicated to St. Martin, of the same period. But it is its church of Notre Dame, to which still clings the name of the cathedral, although the bishopric was suppressed during the Revolution (1789), which is the principal object of attraction in Laon, and it is of this building that Boys gives us a partial view in the accompanying illustration.

It appears that a former church existed on this site, dating from the later part of the eleventh century or perhaps earlier. This structure was, however, destroyed by fire in 1112, and, soon after, the present church, one of the most important in the northern part of France, was begun. Its completion did not take place till well into the following century.

It was thoroughly and carefully restored, "recently," says one authority writing in the eighties, but happily its characteristic features were preserved both in renovation and addition, and so the magnificent façade, one of the great pieces of pure Gothic in existence, with its two graceful towers, remains in

7. *Laon Cathedral*

appearance much as it must have been when its early builders completed it. These two west towers can be seen in the distance in Boys's picture, the porch shown in the foreground being that on the south of the building.

As we can only dimly discern, in the accompanying picture, the two west towers, let me quote what the faithful Baedeker has to say about them : " The lower part of these towers is square, the upper octagonal, while above the buttresses at the angles rise belfries of two stories, adorned on the second story with figures of oxen, in memory of the animals who dragged the stones of the cathedral from the plain to the site of the building. It was originally intended to erect two similar towers at each end of the transepts, but only three of these have been completed." The architecture of these towers is remarkable for its detached clustering columns, with animals looking out as from cages.

The interior of the church possesses many interesting features ; but I cannot enlarge on these here, as it would take up too much space, and would, after all, hardly be in place in an account which is chiefly based on the exterior of the fabric as seen by the artist when he made his drawing.

The church was originally connected with a range of conventual buildings on an extensive scale, and Boys also notes that some of the houses in the adjoining streets exhibited grotesque heads carved on corbels which were once probably part and parcel of these monastic remains.

The picture, as usual with the artist, is an exceedingly careful rendering of a very attractive subject ; and we can even distinguish one of the Norman pillars of the Cathedral's transept through the open doorway. An air of activity noticeable among the figures introduced probably indicates that it is a market-day. In contradiction to Boys's usual custom the picture is unsigned.

IT is possible that of the thousands who yearly pass to and fro through Abbeville on their way to Paris or the coast, relatively few have stopped at the town on the Somme. The Great War, of course, opened up the place to numbers to whom it had hitherto been but a name, but that was not a time particularly conducive to the study of the picturesque in any form, much less when architectural and pictorial beauties were being ruthlessly destroyed, and men had to think of preserving their own lives before they could be expected to spend time in examining the relics which antiquity had left us.

In the circumstances, especially as Boys's beautiful picture does not happen to contain any special historical landmark requiring elucidation, it seems worth while to set down such notable facts in Abbeville's records as may help to show that it was a place of importance in its day. It was the ancient capital of Ponthieu, and so early as the time of Hugh Capet, who was King of France from 987 to 996, it was regarded as sufficiently important to be strongly fortified by encircling ramparts. Here it was that the leaders of the first and second Crusades forgathered, and the preaching of Peter the Hermit and Peter the Penniless must have been heard in its streets ; while the magnetic personality of Godfrey de Bouillon could have been seen often enough in the place where, fifty years later, St. Bernard preached the less successful second crusade of 1147.

But Abbeville has for the English a closer connection even than the Crusades (for our Richard I. was associated only with the third of these) in the fact that when Edward I. married Eleanor of Castile it passed into his possession. That was in 1272, and for nearly a couple of centuries it remained the property of the English Crown. Towards the close of the fifteenth century, however, it became subject to the Dukes of Burgundy, but soon after the death of Charles the Bold, at the Battle of Granson in 1476, it reverted to France. The place is notable, too, as having been the scene of the wedding festivities of Louis XII. and Mary Tudor, the sister of Henry VIII., in 1514, while just thirteen years later the pact between England and France against Charles V. of Spain was here signed by Francis I. and Cardinal Wolsey, three years before the disgrace and death of the latter. It will thus be seen that Abbeville has through the ages been in specially close connection with this country, and should, therefore, have a more than ordinary interest for English visitors.

As in the case of nearly every large town in France, the town possesses all sorts of interesting features, the most noticeable in this case being the Church of St. Wulfram, which was begun in 1488, and unfortunately not completed till the seventeenth century, when a debased style did much to spoil the beauty of the earlier design. It is probably the most outstanding example of architectural flamboyance, and, as such, is an object-lesson—in what direction different tastes will suggest. It was dedicated to St. Wulfram, who was once Bishop of Sens, and whose relics were first brought to Abbeville in the year 1205. The effective façade is flanked by two towers, which can be seen behind the trees in Boys's picture. The cathedral possesses a triple portal, once decorated by statues,

8. *Rue de Rivage, Abbeville*

many of which have disappeared. There are, too, some interesting buttresses as well as a couple of galleries with balustrades outside. The interior is rather disappointing, owing partly to the narrowness of the nave and the fact that the choir was, curiously enough, only formed in the last, and debased, period of the church's erection. Of the chapels, that of Notre Dame des Merciers, at the end of the south aisle, is the most noticeable, to some extent on account of the great gilded Gothic canopy, beyond which a statue of the Madonna may be seen. There is another church here dedicated to St. Gilles, and possessing a fine doorway in the Flamboyant style. Boys, in his short note accompanying the picture, does not, of course, enter into all these details, but he tells us that Abbeville takes its name from a villa of the Abbey of St. Riquier ; that its site is low and damp owing to its vicinity to the river ; and that it possessed in his time many old wooden houses, which were both dirty and dilapidated. As I have said, the majority of people know Abbeville because of being carried through it by train. In the artist's day they posted, and were accustomed to descend here for a greater or less length of time, the consequence being that the early nine-teenth-century traveller knew the place probably better than does the twentieth.

Although the town is not so important as some of which Boys has given us his exquisite glimpses, the artist has here produced one of his most attractive pictures. The collocation of buildings and trees, and, above all, the presence of water, make the work more of a complete artistic composition than was often possible in other cases. One feels somehow that Boys must have executed it in complacent, and even merry, mood, for he has not merely signed it, but has taken on an alien calling in doing so ; and thus we read on the sign of the shop in the right-hand foreground the words : " T. Boys, Aubergiste "!

THOSE who know Rouen are acquainted with the Museum which stands almost in the centre of the city facing the Rue Thiers, and those who know the Museum have seen the Church of St. Laurent which is situated on its east side masking another sacred edifice, St. Godard, lying behind it. When a place like Rouen possesses an outstanding ecclesiastical feature, the visitor, unless he is making a stay, is apt to overlook smaller ones, and so it is possible that, although the exterior of St. Laurent and St. Godard may be glanced at, the sightseer has time perhaps only for the cathedral, St. Ouen, the Hotel de Ville next to it, and the Musée, in which may be seen so many interesting pictures and a few exquisite examples of ancient and modern art.

The Church of St. Laurent is not one over which the much-exercised Baedeker or Murray can afford to spend superfluous descriptive energy. Indeed, all that the former was wont to say about it was that it dated from the fifteenth and sixteenth centuries, and possessed an interesting tower, which is just one of those provocative sentences which, I suppose, really indicate the use of a guide-book and justify its publication. As a matter of fact, Rouen is not a place where such an aid to knowledge should be necessary—except, of course, as an incentive to curiosity, which can alone properly satisfy itself amid the relics and architectural features of the city. For it is so famous a city that it takes its place amid mediæval towns by the side, though in a far less important character, of course, of Rome and Perugia and Florence. The feature with which Boys here presents us is that portion of the Church of St. Laurent which, as I have said, the guide-books dismiss with the much-used and convenient word, "interesting."

St. Laurent, a fine example of late Gothic, was begun, on the site of an earlier church burnt down in 1248, in or about the year 1400, but not completed till 1501. Originally the elevation of the tower here shown was much greater than it now is. The fact is that many of its higher pinnacles were destroyed by successive storms in 1520 and again in 1677, no less than ten feet being on one occasion carried away by a tempest. Over the principal entrance is a balustrade of carved and pierced work representing in Gothic characters the words from the book of Job :

"Post Tenebras spero Lucem."

During the French Revolution the church was made use of for meetings of the Société Populaire, whose sittings were held in this unaccustomed environment. Boys, who records this fact, also makes the following statement : " It is now (*circa* 1839) in the occupation of a wheelwright; a long chimney-flue reaches across the choir, and coaches, waggons, and diligences block up the interior of the nave "; so that even in the artist's time the desecration of the sacred edifice continued ; and in more recent times we know that the lower stages of the tower were used as lodgings, and that the body of the church had been converted into shops and furniture warehouses ! The building shown in

9. *St. Laurent, Rouen*

front of the church was at this time used as a convent, one of its prominent features being a gargoyle which projects well from the wall. On the old tumble-down houses on the right will be observed a beautifully carved niche. Such features as this are frequently to be found happily preserved even where rebuilding has eradicated all other signs of the *Moyen Age*. A large and prosperous place like Rouen cannot, of course, be expected to keep *in situ* much of this kind of work, as smaller places, like Blois and Amboise and so forth, have been able to do. But Rouen has many attractive features besides its ecclesiastical remains. It has, for instance, its memories of Pierre Corneille, who was born here, and whose birthplace, No. 4, Rue de Corneille, can still be seen ; and a few miles outside the city, his dwelling-place at Petit Couronne, now the property of the State. Then there is the Place de la Pucelle, the spot where Joan of Arc is traditionally said to have been burned by the English in 1431. There were plenty of witches burnt in France as well as in England in those days, to the delight of a brutalized and ignorant people, and it is scarcely surprising that Joan should have been regarded as one, in having effected the miraculous things her influence and splendid courage made possible. Twenty years after her death Rome asserted by a Papal Bull that she was not a witch ; and a cross to her memory was set up here. In a sense, therefore, " the Maid " is Rouen's most precious memory, and even Corneille's fame fades before that splendid example of faith and courage.

The latest writer on Rouen, speaking specifically of St. Laurent, of whose history, by the way, nothing is said, remarks (1899) that " once used as a magazine of shops of every kind, sometimes a lost home for decrepit carriages, sometimes a drying-house for laundry women, these exquisite ruins of Renaissance architecture have at last been rescued by the civic authorities, if not from evident decay, at any rate from further mutilation," and adds truly enough that " the tower alone—but one among so many in Rouen—would be the proudest possession of many a larger English town."

ROUEN has sometimes been called "The Manchester of France," but these comparisons are generally found, on investigation, to be half-truths masquerading as whole ones. In this case, the fact that the cotton industry is common to both places is about the sole ground for the statement; and, notwithstanding much alteration and rebuilding, Hugo's phrase that it is essentially "la ville aux vieilles rues" still to a great extent holds good. For its old gabled houses, rickety with age and romance; its exquisite corners, known and dear to innumerable artists; its more outstanding landmarks, the Palais de Justice, the Hotel Bourgthéroulde, the cathedral with its marvellous mediæval staircase, and, perhaps more famous than all, its great clock sprawling across the roadway, make up a collocation of interesting and attractive features, which, so far as my limited knowledge of Manchester is concerned, is no more like what one sees in that busy city than the proverbial chalk is like the proverbial cheese. And this is not necessarily to decry Manchester, the stately buildings of which city have an impressiveness and dignity of their own; but it is not, as it happens, the impressiveness conferred by age, or of that kind which is obvious to all in the French town.

But, curiously enough, both places date from Roman times, ours being known as a manufacturing centre in the fourteenth century. But whereas Rouen's development in commerce went hand in hand with exquisite artistry, Manchester's artistic development can hardly be said to be of an older growth than the nineteenth century, when it first emerged as the patron of so many artists of our own day. In a word, the artistic qualities of the French town were inherent; those of the English were imported.

But it is of Rouen alone that one has here to say something, and that special something is concerned with what for most people is its most outstanding and familiar feature—its great clock. Such a landmark as this is not, of course, unique. There are not dissimilar ones at Berne, Vire, and elsewhere; but the Rouen example is of such a special character in its size, design, and position, that it has properly become world-renowned.

This clock, with its architectural appurtenances, standing in the street as it does, may not inaptly be termed the Temple Bar of Rouen. It is a delightfully characteristic scene which Boys here presents to us. First, there is the "Sight's Self," from which the busy street takes its name, with its amazing dial on which not merely the minutes and the hours are marked, but also the days and months, by zodiacal signs—a clock not merely to tell the hours, but the years of a man's life; to tick off the fleeting minutes and the days with something of the awful insistence of that sinister time-piece on which Baudelaire wrote his famous lines.

Neither the maker's name nor the date of Rouen's Grosse Horloge is known, although it is recorded as being in existence at the beginning of the fifteenth century. How it was then supported we are not told, but it is a fact that the archway which now bears it was not erected till the year 1527.

Another feature in Boys's picture is the tower which rises on the left-hand

10. *Rue de la Grosse Horloge, Rouen*

side.   This is the belfry to which the clock really belongs, and the bell in the turret above the dome is called " Raimbold," and is popularly known as the silver bell on account of its clear and argentine notes.   It was used for tolling the curfew at nine o'clock, and also for fire alarms ; and during the Revolution its " tocsin " must have spread terror in many hearts.   In public rejoicings it also had its share.   Indeed, it has fulfilled—and, I suppose, still fulfils—as many services in this way as are enumerated by Poe in his well-known verses.   Its notes are always silvery in tone, but to many they could hardly have sounded as euphonious as the term implies.

Boys, as was his custom, does not restrict himself merely to the architectural features in his picture.   He introduces the life of the streets in a variety of forms, and here with a background of old houses leaning over with age, as if a little tired of standing so long, we have the people of Rouen driving and walking about, as the artist saw them there eighty odd years ago.   We note, too, that one P. Turpin had his piano factory in a house next door to Rupert the tailor ; that elsewhere Paragon et Tournon kept their shop ; while, with his wonted humour, the artist inscribes on yet another wall the legend " T. Boys, Vidangeur." The cabriolet dashing down the street gives an air of movement and life, curiously alien to the calm front of the fine eighteenth-century building on the right-hand foreground, with the arms impressed on its side, at the corner of the Rue Timouret, where the two women are seated amid their cans and vegetables.

THE accompanying picture possesses great artistic qualities, and is not one of the least successful of Boys's productions. The depth of colouring in the green trees placed in apposition to the deep slate of the roof of the garden house; the glimpse of blue sky between the clouds; the dilapidated but picturesque old building, sole remains of what must once have been an ecclesiastical establishment of considerable size and importance; the group of old women and children in the foreground, the ladders and wheels, and the chickens pecking about, all help to form a charming and characteristically French picture, the composition of which the artist has obviously made a labour of love.

The trouble is that Boys, who, as I have said elsewhere, contributed the scantiest of scanty notes to his lithographs, has failed to give us much information about the ruin in these slight written accompaniments to his pictures. Nor do the few facts he does present us with tell us very much. However, I am able to supplement these data by the following information. The Abbaye de St. Amand, which stands near the Hotel de France, close by the Priory of St. Lô, was founded in or about the year 1030, and was richly endowed by Robert, Duke of Normandy; but whether this Robert was the duke popularly surnamed "the Devil," who died in 1035, or Robert II., the son of William the Conqueror, who expired in prison just upon a century later, we are not informed, although it is more likely that it was the former. Its dedication took place with much solemnity in 1070. Successive monarchs of France are said to have given special honour to the place, of which, in Boys's time, so little remained that he can only speak of it as consisting of a heterogeneous mass of buildings of various styles and ages, inhabited by a motley assemblage of tenants. As a matter of fact, the Abbaye de St. Amand, such as it was in Boys's time and as it practically remains today, is not that of the eleventh century at all, for there is hardly a stone existing which can be traced with certainty to that period; and what we see now, and what the artist saw, are the remains of the structure, as it was rebuilt in 1274, the tower of which was reconstructed so much later as 1570. It is interesting to know that the last Abbess, Madame de Lorge, died in 1745; and that one of those corporations, or trade guilds, which were accustomed to associate themselves with different religious fraternities, that of the "Savetiers," joined the *confrèrie* of the Holy Trinity at St. Amand.*

The interior, we are told, contained some fine oak-panelling and certain decorations in the Arabesque style. In fact, its greatness is as much in the past as, to take a solitary instance from our own country, the once magnificent and powerful Llanthony Abbey in Gloucester (not to be confounded with its Welsh offshoot) is today, when railway sidings and trucks run over its site, and nothing remains to attest its former splendour but an archway and a coat of arms.

In the dearth of reliable information concerning this Abbaye de St. Amand

---

* St. Amand is not classed among the places taken over by the Government as Historic Monuments of France.

11. *L'Abbaye St. Amand, Rouen*

at Rouen, I may mention the fact that there is another place of the same name to the north of Valenciennes, situated on the railway between that town and Lille, the track running through the Forest of St. Amand and the coal-fields of Vicogne. Here there was an abbey, but of far earlier date than that pictured by Boys, for the Valenciennes one is said to have been founded as early as the seventh century by St. Amand himself. This St. Amand is sometimes called St. Amand-les-Eaux, on account of its hot springs, which possess mineral properties.*

But, according to the recognized description of its ruined abbey, " nothing remains except the portal and the façade of the church, the latter a bold construction in the Renaissance style, consisting of a tower and two turrets, said to have been designed by Rubens."

The trained artistic eye of a man like Boys recognized in this little collocation of buildings a picturesque subject. He no doubt realized, too, that a " find " is often more pleasing, even if it be of a relatively insignificant thing, than the perpetuation of what is known to all as a masterpiece. Otherwise, being in Rouen, of which, as we have seen, he has given us other views, it is strange that he did not set down, in terms of his art, some of the beauties, say, of St. Ouen, a sacred edifice, larger in extent and even finer in style than the cathedral itself ; or of St. Patrice, with its wonderful stained glass ; or of St. Maclou, notable for its florid Gothic. In fact, there are numberless points of interest in Rouen which Boys might well have selected. But he chose, as it happened, something which intrigues at least one humble admirer of his work, for that admirer sees in this picture a delightful " composition," but for the life of him cannot with any certainty annotate it in this note, as he would like to do.

The lithograph is signed T. Boys, and is dated 1839.

* There is yet another St. Amand in France, known alternatively as St. Amand-Montrond, situated in the Department of Cher, about twenty-five miles south-east of Bourges.

As you go up the Boulevard St. Michel, the "Boul Mich" of Murger's Quartier Latin, from the river, you see on your left some ancient buildings enclosed in a railed-off garden in which fragments of old stone are dotted about. The first turning on the left is the Rue du-Sommerard, bounded by the wall of the Hotel Cluny, in which Boys sat when he made his sketch for the accompanying lithograph. It is interesting, parenthetically, to remember that eastward from where it intersects the Rue St. Jacques, the Rue du-Sommerard is modern and passes over the sites successively of the Commanderie of St. Jean de Latran, and the ancient colleges of Beauvais and de Presles. In early days this street was known as the Rue des Mathurins-St. Jacques, and in still older times (the thirteenth century) as the Rue du Palais des Thermes. The present name of the street was bestowed on it in 1867, to commemorate the great collector who founded the Museum.

The Musée de Cluny stands on the site of the Roman Palais des Thermes (hence the early name of its adjacent street) where Julian was actually proclaimed Emperor in 360. Indeed, the place was inhabited by various Roman rulers and by some of the French kings "de la première race," as they are termed. In the time of Philippe VI., a certain Pierre de Chaslus, then Abbot of Cluny, purchased the existing remains of this old palace, and in its place began the beautiful Gothic edifice of which a certain portion still remains, and of the gateway of which Boys has left us the accompanying picture. Chaslus dying, his successor, Jean de Bourbon, carried on the work, it being completed in 1490 by Jacques d'Amboise, whose crest, a pilgrim's cockle-shell, can still be seen on the walls. The succeeding abbots, however, appear to have had so little use for the building that they let it to various people, among the first tenants being Mary of England, sister of our Henry VIII., and widow of Louis XII., "la reine blanche," as she was called from the fact that she wore white mourning. As is well known she became the wife, *en secondes noces*, of the Duke of Suffolk; and the story goes that Francis I. suddenly finding the pair in a somewhat compromising situation here, insisted on their being there and then married by the Cardinal who happened to accompany him on his visit. Later, a company of actors took up their quarters here in 1579, and opened a theatre in the precincts. Among other inhabitants was the famous Cardinal de Lorraine; his nephew the Duc de Guise, the Papal Nuncio, in 1610; and the Abbess of the Port-Royal-des-Champs, in 1625.

It need hardly be said that during the Revolution the property, having passed into the hands of the authorities—in other words, having been confiscated under the specious pretext of the public good—fell on bad times. One of the "sections" held its meetings here; the great hall served as the workshop of a barrel-maker; then it became a laundry, until, by a decree of Napoleon, dated 1807, it was converted into a hospital. The lovely chapel was divided, and the dwelling-house, where princes of the Church and royal personages had lived, degenerated into furnished lodgings for anyone who could afford the trifling

12. *Hotel Cluny, Paris*

rent asked, other portions of the building being used as a printing office. By great good luck, however, Mons. du-Sommerard, a collector of beautiful and rare things and an enlightened antiquary, was able to acquire the place as a home for this wonderful assemblage of works of art of the *Moyen Age* and the Renaissance which he had accumulated. At his death the Beaux Arts purchased the collection for a relatively small sum, owing to the public spirit of his heirs, and in 1843 the Government bought the Hotel Cluny itself from its then proprietress, Madame Le Prieur. A few years earlier the hospital had, too, been bought out ; and in 1844 the Musée de Cluny, more or less as it is now, was opened to the public. Today, as everybody knows, it is one of the show places of Paris, and practically every visitor to the city goes there as a matter of course. Taken in conjunction with the Musée Carnavalet, it represents a complete picture of the various epochs of the country from the Middle Ages down to these days of Napoleon III., as exemplified in the furniture and decorative objects of that long period.

In the picture before us we have a representation of the outer entrance of the building as it appeared in the days of Louis Philippe. What a marked difference there was between that time and ours, in regard to such things, is shown by the fact that the walls of one of the most exquisite of Renaissance buildings, and one, too, at that time inhabited by so great a collector and antiquary as Du-Sommerard, were permitted to be defiled by innumerable bills, from the official " Lois et Actes Publiques " to those of private enterprise, as indicated in the notice of " Sinet, Brocheur Satineur." No wonder Boys humorously signs himself on a bill close by " T. Boys, Farceur."

By the way, the jade-green of which the artist was so fond, and which is said to distinguish the plates of the *London Views* coloured by himself, is here seen used for the wooden doorway around which the beautiful, but here and there dilapidated, Renaissance stonework runs.

THIS picture forms a companion to the preceding one. There we were outside the entrance-gate; here we are within the courtyard of M. Du-Sommerard's treasure-house, a treasure-house which, under the able direction of M. Haracourt, has become in our times a Mecca for those who are interested in Mediæval and Renaissance objects, or who are lovers of the beautiful for itself without a knowledge or thought of " periods." Boys has indulged here in a sly touch of humour by writing up " Du-Sommerard, Brocanteur " on one of the walls. And, by the way, it is not amiss in this place to remark that, in examining pictures of this artist, one should not overlook any of these mural adornments, for they often have a special significance, and sometimes throw interesting sidelights on the subjects. Thus, had one not known all about M. Du-Sommerard's connection with the Hotel Cluny, and what kind of man he was, the name thus set up would have conveyed no particular significance, and one might easily have supposed the owner to have been a simple " brocanteur " who had taken advantage of municipal indifference and a neglected wall to advertise himself. The artist has taken, too, the opportunity afforded him, in including the name in his picture, to introduce the figure of the man on the ladder, who is apparently putting the final touches to the inscription.

If you enter the courtyard today you will recognize little difference in its appearance from that which it presents in the picture before us. It is tidier and has more of an official air, perhaps. But there is the beautiful over-doorway; there are the cockle-shells and staff, indicating its former abbatial character, carved on the wall; there are the escutcheons and devices of the Amboise family over the windows; and there are the four ogival arcades on the left of the entrance, as they were in Boys's time. I have frequently been in the place, but I am not sure whether there can still be traced, as was formerly the case, the circumference of the famous Georges d'Amboise's clock, which was once in the courtyard, and was destined for the cathedral of Rouen.

The whole effect of the architecture of the building is that fascinating one which comes from the admixture of the early French and the Italian Renaissance; the rather flamboyant superimposition on a restrained background which produces such charming and interesting results. The very incompleteness of these remains helps us to appreciate them. We see what is gone, and realize how lucky we are to possess what is left; for completion overlooks the possibility of loss, and one is apt to be careless of, or ungrateful for, what one has. That, perhaps, is why a ruin is somehow so often more attractive than an unspoiled relic.

As usual, Boys links up these treasures of the past with something vital. Here we have the human element in the form of the man playing the hurdy-gurdy, with two youngsters listening to the sounds. One sympathizes with their pleasure, but one cannot but help feeling that indoors M. Du-Sommerard is putting his fingers in his ears or tearing his hair!

On the right of the building before us, and spreading around it on the other side, is the garden, which was not actually formed till 1856, at the time, indeed,

13. *Hotel Cluny—The Courtyard*

when the Hotel Cluny was made one with the remains of the old Palais des Thermes. In this garden are a number of interesting monumental remains, although they give one rather the idea of a stonemason's yard which has not quite made up its mind to get transformed into a cemetery. There may be seen the doorway of the Chapel of the Virgin attached to the Abbey St. Germain-des-Prés, the work of the famous P. de Montereau ; the pinnacle of the chapel of the Château de Vincennes ; and the doorway of the Benedictine monastery of Argenteuil.

To say anything adequate about the richness and variety of the contents of the Museum itself is obviously impossible here. Much of what we see there today was inside it when Boys sat making his sketch (on which, by the by, he has placed his signature over the doorway), but much has since been added. From sculpture and painting to old slippers and instruments of torture, nothing seems wanting to form a picture for us of the days when men went to war in plate-armour and ladies wore those tall headdresses called Henins which would have made a journey in a close carriage, had such then existed, an impossibility. There are ivories here which are marvels of ingenious workmanship, and enough keys, if they but fitted, to open, or so one imagines, all the doors of Paris ; and here, too, are those notorious " ceintures " which most people look at while modestly affecting not to see them.

IN a fork formed by the Rue de l'Hotel de Ville and the Rue du Figuier, and having its entrance facing the Rue des Barrès (now the Rue de l'Ave Maria) stood the famous Hotel de Sens. A fragment still exists of this structure, and Boys here gives us a delightful and, as usual, an accurate picture of it. Even in its truncated form it is one of the most remarkable specimens of fifteenth-century architecture surviving in Paris.

In 1296, during the reign of Philippe le Bel, Étienne Becquard established the first official residence of the Archbishops of Sens in Paris, purchasing from Pierre Marcel, uncle of the famous Étienne Marcel, a house on the site of which the École Massillon now stands, on the Quai des Celestins. Not long, however, did this structure remain the property of the Church, for, about the year 1364, Charles V. converted it into a royal palace, known as the Hotel de Saint Pol. In exchange for this confiscation, the King gave to the Archbishopric of Sens the Hotel d'Hestomesnil, in front of which stood the Poor-house, which Louis IX. (St. Louis) had founded in 1230. About a century later this Hotel d'Hestomesnil became ruinous. At this time Tristan de Salazar was the Archbishop of Sens, and, being a man of artistic character, he undertook the reconstruction of his archiepiscopal residence, on such beautiful and gracious lines as to make it one of the most attractive structures in Paris. Tristan, a worthy son of his father, who, a valiant Spanish soldier of fortune, had aided Charles VII. against the English, and who is said to have saved the life of Louis XI. at the Battle of Montlhéry, had accompanied Louis XII. in his Italian campaigns, and appears not to have been above collecting artistic loot for the embellishment of his Paris residence. It would seem that at his death, in 1519, the Hotel de Sens was still unfinished, for his successor, Antoine Du Prat—afterwards raised to the Cardinalate—when visiting Paris, is known to have stayed in other quarters. However, it was certainly here that, in 1528, he assembled the Concile de Sens, as it was called, which had for its object the condemnation of Luther and all his works. Soon after Du Prat's death, however, the place became a regular residence, and assumed a sort of quasi-royal, quasi-religious character.

The first of its more famous occupants was Louis de Bourbon, the grandfather of Henri Quatre; then came Jean Bertrand, successively President of the Parliament of Paris and Ambassador to Venice, who entered into the religious order after the death of his wife; then Louis de Lorraine, better known as the Cardinal de Guise, and vulgarly called, not without reason, " le cardinal des bouteilles." He died here in 1568, " ayant," as a French writer expresses it, " beaucoup aimé les arts—et l'art culinaire en particulier," and was followed by the Cardinal de Pellevé, one of the protagonists of the Ligue, who is familiar to those who know the "Satyre Ménippée," and who died of chagrin on learning that Henri Quatre had entered Paris in triumph after the Battle of Ivry. His successor was that amazing gourmand, Renaud de Beaune, of whose gastronomic powers—powers almost equalling those of Louis XVIII. and the Duc Décazes—such extraordinary stories are told. In 1605, however, this personage, although

14. *Hotel de Sens, Paris*

in Paris, was not, for some reason, occupying the Hotel de Sens, eating, indeed, his continual meals and taking his continual *siestas* at the Collège de Navarre (where the École Polytechnique is now), and so, when Marguerite de Valois, the repudiated wife of Henri Quatre, wished to stay in Paris, the King arranged for her to do so here.

It was in the space before the gates that, in the following year, the Comte de Vermond was executed for having killed Dal de St. Julien, a favourite page of the Queen. Furious at the latter's murder, Marguerite swore that she would neither eat nor drink till she had seen justice done on his assassin, and the day after the crime, April 6, 1606, Vermond paid the penalty. Marguerite thereupon left the Hotel de Sens, when Renaud de Beaune returned to it, and here died, to be followed in residence by Cardinal Duperron. Soon after, in 1623, the bishopric of Sens gave up the place, and it was let once to Philippe de Dreux, conseilleur du roi; then to Denys Feydeau; still later to M. de Meaupeou; and at last as the headquarters of the "Lyons Mail," familiar to us through the play founded on the subject. In 1830, during the Revolution, a cannon-ball struck one of the walls and was imbedded there. In course of time a sweet-stuff shop was opened here, and still later Harroux, an ironmonger, occupied it—to such uses had come the one-time home of princes.

Boys's view is taken from the Rue des Barrés, so called, by the way, from the house of a religious fraternity here, whose members wore striped gowns, and whose sign-plate is still on the left of the entrance. Close by, the words "29 Juillet, 1830" are seen inscribed, indicating the spot where the bullet—the mark of which can be discerned in the centre of the gable—entered the wall. It was during an attack on the Caserne de la Vierge Marie, in this street, that the Hotel de Sens was itself hit, and not owing to any special offensive against that place itself. The tricolour hanging over the entrance might be supposed to show that the hotel was a national possession, but I rather think Boys has placed it there to indicate that the national flag was then flying from a spot more naturally associated with the fleur-de-lis. But Louis Philippe was on the throne when the picture was executed, and he made a point of being the Patriot King, and was always ready to exhibit the emblem of the sovereignty of the people, as if it were that of his own dynasty. The life of the streets is shown by the man with the hand-barrow carrying a trunk and other luggage; the man with the cart bearing the wine-tub has probably just left the wine shop with the sign of "Au St. Esprit."

The picture is signed (on the left-hand side of the central doorway) "T. Boys," and those who know the lithograph which Rouargue produced of the Hotel de Sens in 1835, can compare it with that here reproduced, and thus see the work of contemporary artists of two nations working on the same subject, and more or less from the same point of view.

ST. SÉVÉRIN, which is by common consent one of the most beautiful and interesting of the Paris churches, stands on the south bank of the river, amid that labyrinth of little streets whose names recall the Middle Ages in which many of them were formed: the Rue de la Hachette; the Rue de Fouarre, which Dante, who was once a student in Paris, mentions; the Rue Chat-qui-Pêche (that tiny byway); the Rue Zacharie, once known as the Rue Sac-à-Lie; the Rue Galande; and the Rue St. Sévérin itself, with the wide and busy Boulevard St. Germain close by, forming one of those marked antitheses which are so noticeable in the half-rebuilt Paris of today. The church, a masterpiece of Gothic, arose on the site of the oratory of Childebert I., which in turn had been built on the spot where St. Sévérin, a solitary of the sixth century, had passed his time in prayer, and where he had been buried. Another saint was to be associated with the place, for it was in Childebert's oratory that St. Cloud, the son of Clodomir, assumed the monastic habit. In 1031 the Normans destroyed the oratory; but in course of time the present church was begun, its building being facilitated by indulgences granted by Pope Clement VI. No one knows who was the architect, but doubtless, as was usual at the time, its gradual accretion of beauties was the work of various designers all labouring in the common task of forming a homogeneous whole. All that investigators have been able to discover is that a certain Michault le Gros directed the construction of the south chapels.

Other portions of the church date from the thirteenth to the sixteenth century, but all preserve that harmony which the architects of the past (though of different periods) always seemed to aim at and achieve. On the porch of the tower can still be read the fifteenth-century inscription, " Bonnes gens qui par cy passées, priez Dieu pour les tréspassés."

The chief entrance is in the Rue Prêtres de St. Sévérin (the street we see in front, in Boys's drawing, is the Rue St. Sévérin), on the right of the picture, and the porch of this entrance is a specially interesting object, for it was originally that of St. Pierre aux Bœufs, one of the eighteen little churches which once clustered round Notre Dame on the Isle de la Cité, and which was destroyed in 1837. The porch on the north is noticeable for another reason, for it was between the two stone lions to be seen here that the priests of St. Sévérin dispensed justice; hence the origin of their decrees being headed " Datum inter leones." There are two outstanding glories of the church: the series of superb windows, most of which came from St. Germain-des-Prés, that much devastated fabric which was once actually threatened with demolition, and was only saved at the intercession of the architect, Petit-Radel; and the series of amazing gargoyles, some of which can be seen in Boys's picture.

A few years ago a very beautiful publication, entitled *Le Vieux Paris*, was issued under the direction of the famous French author, M. Lenotre. It deals with outstanding historical and architectural features of the city, and the first chapter is concerned with an account of St. Sévérin, written by M. Lucien

15. *Church of St. Séverin, Paris*

Lambeau. The illustrations in photogravure are exceptionally fine, and enable us to realize the charm of the church from all sides, as well as some of the detail work, notably the gargoyles and the façade on the garden front—the façade, that is, at the back of the structure as we are here looking at it. There are few things more characteristic of the fantastic decoration of ecclesiastical work of the Middle Ages than the gargoyle, and here at St. Sévérin they are seen in the highest expression of their whimsical and often allegorical significance. As you pass down the Rue St. Sévérin (where Boys took his stand when executing this delightful picture) you look up and see a series of ten of these weird projections stretching out their elongated necks and, as it were, regarding you with that half-baleful, half-satirical gaze which exemplifies so much of the life of the *Moyen Age*.

There is no necessity, even had I the space, here to enlarge on the architectural features of the interior of this fascinating church. Those who know it, and there can be few visitors to Paris who do not, will remember how curiously the little votive tablets, set up by grateful students of the neighbouring *Lycées* for success in their examinations, which cover so much of the wall-space, link up our days with the mediævalism elsewhere dominant. They will know, too, the beautiful little underground Chapelle des Catéchismes, and the Vicar's house, formerly known as Les Charniers ; but they may not be acquainted with the fact that the church was once the headquarters of the Jansenists down to 1820, that it was used as a powder magazine in 1794, and that it was Napoleon who, in 1802, reopened it as a place of worship. The first operation for lithotomy is said to have been performed, and to have been successful, in the garden of the church—a strange operating-room indeed ; and the great musician, Saint-Saëns, was once St. Sévérin's famous organist.

Boys's lithograph of this exquisite relic of a past age, whose features on the east and north, by the way, were partly revealed by the pulling down of surrounding houses in 1907, and by still more recent improvements, speaks for itself. It was a subject after his own heart, and he has left us, as usual, a vivid and accurate delineation of it. Apart from the church itself, the artist shows us something of the Paris of his day : the group of children on the steps ; the two priests talking to the boy (an acolyte in mufti probably) ; and on the left foreground the two women gossiping at the entrance to a shop, over which the sign " Cave à Louer " appears ; the man with the load on his back, perhaps a chiffonier ; and the lamp suspended across the street, all make up a vivid and animated picture in apposition to the silent monument looking down upon them from the past. Boys, in this instance, has signed the picture with his initials only, and these can be seen on the post by which one of the women is seated.

ITS doorways are among the most precious portions of Notre Dame. The three splendid ones at the west end; the central one, with its representation of the Day of Judgment; that under the north tower dedicated to the Virgin; that under the south tower known as the Porte Ste. Anne, as well that of St. Stephen on the south side of the cathedral; and the two on the north, the larger of which is called the Porte du Cloître; and finally, further east, the Porte Rouge, which Boys here so carefully delineates. This doorway, which was constructed by Jean de Chelles in 1257 as a choristers' entrance, is notable for the excellent preservation of the figures which adorn it, and which date from the early years of the thirteenth century. In the tympanum (the technical term for the triangular niche between the lintel and the arch) the Coronation of the Virgin is represented; while in the archivolt (the under-curve of the arch from one pillar to the other) are six scenes from the life of St. Marcel. These remarkable sculptures, carved in the deepest relief, are here portrayed by Boys with his usual mastery.

From the student's point of view, such pictures as this are of the highest value, because one knows how accurately the details are copied, and also because one can tell at a glance what state these sculptured figures were in ninety years ago. The Porte Rouge is smaller than the other doors of Notre Dame, but it yields to none in the ecclesiastical and artistic value of its decorative carvings. There is something in its upper portion that reminds one of the exquisite over-doorway fronting the Ponte Paradiso at Venice, while readers of Hugo's *Notre Dame* will remember the prominent place it takes in that romance. The priest watching the two boys feeding a dog, in the foreground, affords the human element in what is otherwise a beautiful representation of petrified religion.

The sketch is signed "T. Boys," but is undated.

(2) *Rue des Marmousets, Paris*

YOU will search long enough in the Paris of today before you find a Rue des Marmousets. Nor even in the old corners of the Cité or the Marais, where here and there still linger, strangely out of keeping with wide streets and Haussmannized boulevards, narrow and dirty byways full of the aura of the *Moyen Age*, and occasionally some piece of sculptured stone, miraculously, as it seems, escaped from the vandals, will you discover such a treasure as Boys has here preserved in terms of art. The artist was lucky in the moment in which he set to work to perpetuate some of the more striking of the picturesque features of the Paris of his day. Much had been destroyed during the Revolution of 1793; something had been desecrated during that of 1830; but in spite of Napoleon I.'s

16. *Rue des Marmousets, Paris*

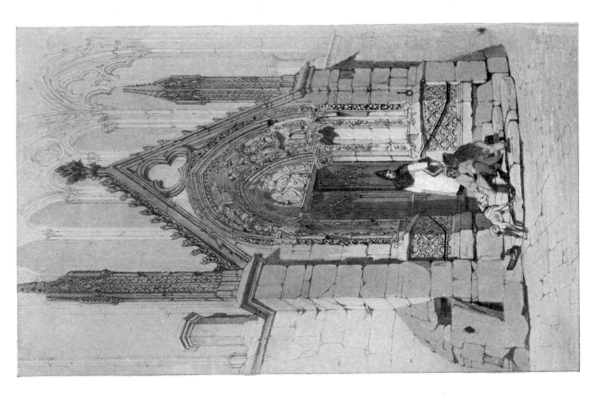

16. *Porte Rouge, Notre Dame, Paris*

plans for a new city, much had been left, especially in the island on which Notre Dame stands.

In those days a collocation of streets and houses almost filled up the space in front of the cathedral, which is now a vast and rather desolate " place." This mass of dwellings and intersecting thoroughfares was, by the way, not very dissimilar from the front of Westminster Abbey in the days before Parliament Square was dreamed of. It was one of these little streets, running north and south, which in those days was known as the Rue des Marmousets, or, as it is written on the sixteenth-century tapestry map, to which I refer elsewhere, Rue des Marmouses. I must leave to etymologists the task of tracing the origin of the name, as well, for the matter of that, of the names of several quaint old streets which, down to the middle of the last century encumbered this spot with picturesqueness and dirt. The Caserne des Sapeurs Pompiers and the Hotel Dieu have obliterated all these relics of the past, and the Rue de Jérusalem (obviously the Jewish quarter), de Pelleterie, dating from 1183, de la Licorne, des Trois Canettes, de Perpignan, Cocatrix, Haut Moulin, and this of the Marmousets disappeared in the holocaust. This Rue des Marmousets, originally known as the Rue des Oublieurs, had a sinister reputation, as its earlier name implies. For, in a house here, a baker, with the connivance and aid of a neighbouring barber, made and sold pâtés compounded of human flesh ! A dog scratching among some débris was the cause of the horrible thing becoming known. The baker's house was situated at the corner of the Rue des Deux-Hermites. It was pulled down, and it was not till the time of Francis I. that anyone was bold enough to erect a dwelling on the sinister spot.

The beautiful doorway here reproduced is of this period, and the salamander on the parapet, the cognizance of Francis I., may indicate that the house was built by the King for one of his mistresses. But, in spite of this rebuilding and regal aura, the memory of the mediæval horror could never, one imagines, get quite eradicated, and Boys, who was a bit of a humorist, may have known the legend, and placed the dog-kennel in the picture as a mute testimony to the fact. If he was conversant with the story, perhaps he had it from the old woman leaning over the balustrade of the steps. I really think he must have been aware of it, the dog-kennel is so appropriate ; but how far more suggestive is that butcher's block and the cleaver sticking vindictively, as it seems, into it. The pots and pans lying about are also, in more senses than one, " in the picture." That picture is, *per se*, a charming one, but one can never, I think, look at it without recalling the horrid deeds " done long ago and ill done " on this site.

Boys has not signed this sketch—perhaps he could not bring himself to do it.

OF all these lithographs I think this is, on the whole, the most beautiful. That it represents what is probably the most perfect architectural monument that even Paris has to show, in no small way accounts for this; but a less accurate and less inspired artist might easily have portrayed this gem-like memorial of France's sainted sovereign (as not a few have done) without catching "the spirit of place" residing in this architectural poem. Exquisite as it is in itself, it is hardly less so in the picture before us. And that picture is, in one way, better than the reality, for notwithstanding that the wondrous chapel is still essentially as it was, although revolutions and turmoils have not respected it, and restoration has had to be resorted to, the beautiful old house on its left is no longer to be seen, and thus Boys has here perpetuated not merely something that, happily, exists, but also something which even by the side of a *chef-d'œuvre* possessed an intimate and appealing charm of its own.

Ste. Chapelle represents the culmination of Gothic art. This wondrous sanctuary has been called by Ruskin "the most precious piece of Gothic in northern Europe," and those who know what Michelet said of it know how he saw a concentration of religious poetry in its lines and in the marvellous tints of its windows, tints, by the way, that gave rise to a once proverbial saying : "Wine of the colour of the windows of Sainte-Chapelle." I must not be led into an essay on Gothic architecture and its significance. The theme is endless, and one might easily become tiresome in tracing it; but in connection with Sainte-Chapelle, I may, perhaps, be allowed to quote what that great authority, Professor Lethaby, has said of the monument of which it is the outstanding feature and the fairest flower. "France not only *led* but *invented*," he writes. "In a very true sense what we call Gothic is Frenchness of the France which had its centre in Paris." Pierre de Montereau (whose name ought to be written in golden letters) conceived this architectural gem in the year 1245, at the desire of St. Louis (Louis IX.), in order that that King should have a fitting shrine in which to place the crown of thorns and the piece of the true cross which he had brought with him from the Crusades. The chapel was completed in three years, and was consecrated in 1248.

At the risk of telling my readers something with which they are already acquainted, I may state that the chapel has two floors, the lower one having been allocated to the royal servants and to those who occupied the neighbouring palace; and the upper one being reserved for the King, for which reason it was constructed on a level with the royal apartments. Apart from the beauty of the architecture and the amazing thirteenth-century windows, which most people know, there is an interesting feature in the interior which may easily be overlooked : it is a little grilled window in the south wall. This was constructed in order that Louis XI., a very different kind of sovereign from his saintly predecessor, although in one respect as great a *dévote*, might see the altar without himself being seen; and one can visualize him, with Peter l'Hermite in attendance, fingering the little leaden figures which adorned his pointed cap, and

74

17. *Ste. Chapelle, Paris*

praying fervently, after coming from Plessis, whose woods he had made hideous with his pendant victims.

One of the features of Sainte-Chapelle, today, is the tall tapering spire which is a landmark from so many points in Paris. It will be observed that this is lacking in Boys's picture. The fact is that in 1630 both it and the roof were destroyed by fire, and the *flèche* was not reconstructed till 1854, during those repairs and renovations which Viollet-le-Duc carried out from 1843 to 1867, and which other devastations during the Revolution, when the chapel was used successively as a club and a barn, had made necessary. When Boys executed his picture, the outside staircase, shining white against the time-worn stones of the chapel itself, had recently been rebuilt.

The beautiful old house with its charming windows, not unreminiscent of our own Inigo Jones, was probably demolished when the adjacent Palais de Justice was erected. On its site was the Chambre des Comptes, built in the time of Louis XII., but burnt down in 1737. Its façade had been designed by the Veronese monk, Fra Giovanni Giacondo. The structure was rebuilt in 1740 ; and Boys's view perpetuates its dignity and charm.

As usual, the artist introduces the human element into his picture, and, as usual, these touches help to give us an idea of the life of the streets, the garments worn, the vehicles and so forth in use. A sentry standing on the left hand and the tricolour flag show the official character of the buildings adjoining Sainte-Chapelle, while the crossed poles and wheel and the masses of stone indicate work proceeding in connection with the Arc de l'Etoile (it is called the Arc de Triomphe now), which was carried on here as being a convenient and little frequented spot ! The lithograph is signed " T. Boys," and is dated 1839.

AS there is no date or signature on this lithograph one can only conjecture that Boys produced the picture from which it is taken about the year 1836, which is the date on one of his water-colours in the Victoria and Albert Museum, depicting the cathedral from nearly, though not quite, the same point of view. The difference between the two is this, that the Museum example is taken *nearer* the edifice, so that the old houses shown on the right in the lithograph are not included. In ancient days the large space in front of Notre Dame was almost entirely filled by houses and narrow streets, the Rue St. Christophe, the Rue Neuve Notre Dame, and so forth. An interesting delineation of this part of Paris in early times is shown in the bird's-eye view executed in tapestry during the sixteenth century, which is preserved in the Bibliothèque Nationale, and to which I have elsewhere referred. Indeed, down to 1868 the Parvis de Notre Dame, as it was called, was but a very small square in front of the west towers of the cathedral. Great buildings like the Hotel Dieu, on the left of the Rue St. Christophe, and the Archbishop's Palace faced it, and were flanked by the smaller structures and streets mentioned. Georges Cain, the late learned curator of the Carnavalet Museum and the writer of many fascinating books on the Paris he knew so intimately, regretted the loss of these encumbrances, " ce décor charmant," as he terms them, and was accustomed to reprehend the action of the authorities which had resulted in converting the area in front of the cathedral into a vast plain, icy in winter and scorching in summer, bounded on one side by a new Hotel Dieu which, as he expressed it, has the appearance of a slaughter-house. One sympathizes with his antiquarian regrets ; but at the same time it must be allowed that the enlargement of the space by the pulling down of old houses and the obliteration of mean streets has resulted in Notre Dame being adequately seen on the west, from a sufficient distance to enable us to judge and appreciate the beauty of its *ensemble* from this direction. This architectural revolution took place in the early eighties of the last century, and today the vast building of the modern Hotel Dieu stretches from the Place du Parvis de Notre Dame (where Charlemagne rides triumphant on his war-horse) to the Quai de la Cité, overlooking the north side of the here-divided Seine, as a small garden does the south branch of the river.

When Boys made his picture he sat among streets and houses that had come down, or had been rebuilt, as the case might be, from the pre-reformed Parvis, and the thoroughfare from which he made his sketch was the Rue Neuve Notre Dame, which had been formed so early as 1163 by Maurice de Sully, when it was known as the Rue St. Geneviève-des-Ardents, from the fact that a chapel of this name stood at its east end facing the cathedral, which chapel came to be known, in course of time, as Notre-Dame-la-Petite. This edifice was destroyed in 1745 after an existence of just over six hundred years, and on its site arose a building which became a Foundling Hospital. This institution existed here till 1838, when it was transferred to the Rue d'Enfer, in the Mont-

18. *Rue Notre Dame, Paris*

parnasse district.   Later it was used as a kind of central bureau for the various Paris hospitals, until its demolition in 1877.   The Rue Notre Dame, which, by the way, was renamed during the Revolution the Rue de la Raison, had disappeared about ten years earlier.

Concerning Notre Dame itself, the chief feature in Boys's picture, there is, of course, here no space to speak at any length, nor, perhaps, in the case of so outstanding and well-known a monument, is it necessary to do so.   I may, however, remind the reader that it was erected on a spot on which a Roman temple, dedicated to Jupiter, had once been, and where, later, Childebert built a church. The first stone of Notre Dame was laid by Pope Alexander III., in 1163, and the structure was completed just eighty-four years later.   Even to mention a tithe of the great ceremonials that have taken place here from the day in 1239 (the church not then being completed) when Louis IX. deposited in it the Crown of Thorns, and that on which the saintly King was buried in 1271, to the sumptuous coronation of Napoleon I. in 1804, and the hardly less sumptuous wedding of Napoleon III. in 1852, is out of the question.   So far as the edifice itself is concerned, one can hardly do better than read the vivid description of it given by Victor Hugo (who knew and loved it so well) in his eponymous work, in order to gain a conception of this wonderful monument as seen through the eye of a poet who was also no little of an antiquary.   Boys's picture of its west front is not merely an artistic and charming study, but it possesses a special value from the fact that the environment of the cathedral here depicted is, today, wholly with the past.   H. Boissard, who sold pots and pans; the purveyor of artists' colours, indicated by the coloured blocks hanging on the house in the foreground; as well as the proprietor of the Patisserie opposite, have long been gathered to their fathers; no more shall you purchase top-boots, or boots of any kind, for the six or seven francs which, as we see, sufficed in the days of Louis Philippe.   You may as soon expect to see in the Paris of these times men hauling trollies along the streets, as you may an oil-lamp slung across the thoroughfare.   By the aid of the artist we are gazing at a little bit of the beautiful city that is as dead as the Dodo, but which by his art seems still to be instinct with the life and activity of these ninety years ago.*   The artist's initials are on the wooden collar of the white horse.

* It is interesting to compare this picture by Boys with a pencil drawing embodying much the same point of view, executed by Henry Edridge, and reproduced in the *Studio* for December, 1920.

THIS is a beautiful rendering of one of Paris's most beautiful churches, just as the situation of the building is one of the most interesting, not only in itself, but because of the antiquity of its surrounding streets.   For instance, the Place Ste. Geneviève, on to which St. Etienne du Mont looks, was in ancient times a Merovingian cemetery.   Later, in the fourteenth century to be precise, it had been converted into an open space known as the Carré Ste. Geneviève, in consequence of the four streets branching from it, up which, by the way, in the first week of January, pilgrims from all parts wend their steps to pray at the shrine of the saintly patroness of Paris.   One of these streets and the most attractive is that on the reader's left hand.   It is known as the Rue de la Montagne-Ste.-Geneviève, and is one of the oldest in Paris.   Not always did it boast its present lengthy name, however, for at the end of the twelfth century it was known as the Rue des Boucheries, and did not change this till 1266. For a few years, 1793 to 1815, when they had not much use for saints, it was called the Rue de la Montagne, *tout court*.

Another little street on the south side of St. Etienne, and dividing it from a block of old buildings, is the Rue St. Etienne du Mont, which used to be the Rue du Moustier as far back as the middle of the thirteenth century, and was, until 1867, known as the Rue des Prêtres-Ste.-Etienne-du-Mont, a name which seems almost longer than the exiguous thoroughfare itself.   On the left-hand side of the picture we see a group of houses, on the nearest one of which can be read the legend : " Pension et Externat.   Classe du Soir.   Table d'Hôte," a pleasant mixture of food for the mind as well as the body, which reminds us that we are here in a distinctly educational as well as ecclesiastical area.   Indeed, both are represented, the former by the Sorbonne, the Lycée Louis le Grand opposite in the Rue St. Jacques, the College St. Barbe in the Place du Pantheon, the Lycée Henri IV. behind that building and on our right (although out of the picture), as we look at St. Etienne, and other colleges close by ; the latter by St. Etienne and the Pantheon themselves.

Other associations of a more tragic character are connected with this area, for it was in an apartment in the Rue de la Montagne-Ste.-Geneviève that Georges Cadoudal, who organized the plot to kill Napoleon I., secreted himself with his accomplices on February 17, 1804, and remained for twenty days in an upper room awaiting intelligence and hiding from Fouché's police, who at length laid them by the heels after a terrible chase and struggle.

One must not loiter about these old streets, however, for all have some interesting relics to reveal or some story to tell, including the Rue de l'Estrapade, on the other side of the Pantheon, which will be forever memorable as the thoroughfare in which Balzac's Maison Vauquer stood, kept by Madame Vauquer (*née* Conflans), and affected by that sinister personage the immortal Vautrin.   Rather must I say something about the church whose fascinating façade is the chief feature of Boys's picture.

In the thirteenth century there was a small chapel, dedicated to St. Etienne,

19. *Church of St. Etienne du Mont, Paris*

on this site, a sort of chapel-of-ease to the neighbouring basilica of Ste. Geneviève. The church which we see here, and which remains today practically as it was then, was begun in the reign of Francis I., but not wholly completed till that of Louis XIII. It is interesting to remember that Marguerite de Valois, whom we have met with at the Hotel de Sens, laid the foundation-stone of the façade in 1610. That façade is remarkable as an example of the fantastic style, and, indeed, may be regarded as a masterpiece of its kind. The back portion of the church, dating from 1517, and the choir, had been built many years—in fact, the latter was finished in 1537; but the whole was not consecrated till 1626. The building had been over a century in getting completed! At first it practically abutted on the old basilica of Ste. Geneviève which stood on its right side where the Rue Clovis runs today, and was, indeed, entered by passing through the older building.

The interior is famous for its double rood-loft of marble, designed by Biard, dividing the choir from the nave; for some excellent windows of wonderfully rich colouring, the work of the famous Pinaigriers; and for its pulpit upheld by Samson with the inevitable jaw-bone in one hand. But, for the devout, " the sight's-self" is the stone on which Ste. Geneviève once reposed (if such a soft word can be used in connection with so hard a substance), which, after vicissitudes during the Revolution, was brought here in 1803, and has been an object of veneration, especially, as I have said, during the first week in January, ever since. The bodies of many great men, including Boileau, Pascal, Descartes, and Racine, have rested at least for a time in the little cemetery behind the church.

Boys made his drawing in 1838 (his signature and the date are on it), and as will be seen he has done full justice to the bizarre but fascinating façade, with its lofty tower and the little perched-up house in which the sacristan has his dwelling. As usual, too, the artist has managed to include some typical figures which, with the flight of pigeons around the tower, give life and movement to it, and seem somehow to revivify the dead stones of its Renaissance builder.

IT is seldom that Boys gives us a night scene. In fact, I know among his work no other example than the one before us. I suspect that he chose it in order to add a certain air of romance to the classicism of the Panthéon in the distance, and was the less concerned in accentuating the details of St. Etienne, inasmuch as he has given us a careful and minute rendering of the amazing façade of that structure in the preceding lithograph in this series. Whatever the reason was, however, there is no doubt that the picture by moonlight is singularly attractive and afforded the artist a striking opportunity for showing his talent in a fresh direction.

We are here looking up the Rue de la Montagne-Ste.-Geneviève with the south side of St. Etienne du Mont facing us, and in the distance the east end of the Panthéon. In the previous note I have said what seemed necessary about the former edifice, and so I can restrict myself to a few details with regard to its classic neighbour which here looms in rather a ghostly way under the light of the moon.

In one of Georges Cain's delightful books about Paris there is an illustration of a ticket entitling the holder to be present at the laying of the foundation-stone of the new church of Ste. Geneviève. The original of this is in the Musée Carnavalet, and the bearer is asked to enter by the Rue de l'Estrapade " vis-à-vis le jeu de paume," which incidentally informs us that a tennis court existed in those days in the street in which Balzac's Madame Vauquer was subsequently to have her pension.

The ceremony took place in the year 1755, when the work on the vast structure was begun. But it was eleven years earlier that the idea for this splendid church first took shape ; and it took shape in the brain of Louis XV. as he lay ill at Metz and when, as we all know from the first graphic chapter of Carlyle's *French Revolution*, " the title of ' Bien-aimé ' had been bestowed on a monarch over whose illness all Paris was mourning and praying, and when, according to President Hénault, the churches resounded with supplications and groans, the prayers of priests and people being every moment interrupted by their sobs." Whether when Louis recovered he was as ready to spend money on this hostage to fortune as when he thought himself dying, is a question ; but certain it is that the bulk of the expense was borne by the aid of three lotteries ! The architect selected was Soufflot (whose name is perpetuated by the street which leads to the west entrance), and he proceeded to erect what was to be the finest classic building in Paris, on the site of an earlier church dedicated to Ste. Geneviève, whose history, by the way, may be read by the curious in Caxton's *Golden Legend*. As the great building arose, the Parisians were delighted with its massive dignity. In 1764 the pillars which were to support the dome were erected, and the work proceeded for many years. But suddenly certain subsidences occurred, and for an awful moment it was feared that the whole structure would come tumbling about the builder's ears. Soufflot was so overwhelmed by the threatened disaster that he died, despairing at once for his masterpiece and

20. *St. Etienne and the Panthéon, Paris*

reputation, and thus leaving his work unfinished. And for a time so it remained. This did not, however, prevent the Constituent Assembly, in 1791, from consecrating it, not to the glory of God but to that of great men, and Camille Desmoulins wrote, in a moment of wonted enthusiasm : " Cette Basilique réunira tous les hommes à sa Réligion "—whatever that religion was supposed to be. In that year Mirabeau's body was placed here, but two years later had to make way for that of " the virtuous Marat," as Joseph Chénier called him. Marat in his turn was ejected a few months later, and in the same year the body of Voltaire was transferred hither, and that of Rousseau three years later, with those full-bodied ceremonies for which the French are famous.

When Napoleon became a power, however, he ordered the building to revert to its original intention, and in 1806 it was handed over to the Archbishop of Paris. Twenty-four years later another revolution again changed it from a church to a Panthéon ; and again in 1850 another Napoleon decreed that it should again become religious in place of being merely monumental. In 1885 it at last became the Panthéon as we know it, and in that year the body of Victor Hugo was placed there, with ceremonies which must, I think (for I happened to witness them), have far outshone even the apotheosis of Voltaire or Rousseau.

The guide-books will tell you that the façade is copied from the eponymous structure at Rome. But the great dome and lateral projections and the sculptures by David D'Angers in the tympanum are apt to make one forget the fact. Inside, the place is rather cold and formal, as most classic structures built on similar lines can hardly fail to be, a coldness and formality that even the coloured decorations of Puvis de Chavannes, Cabanel, Laurens, Bonnat, and, rather unexpectedly, Détaille, are hardly able to counteract. Rodin's " Penseur " sits now in front of the façade, and if he thinks of the vicissitudes of the edifice, he may well appear bemused.

Boys, of course, gives us here but a glimpse of Soufflot's great work ; for it is the south side of St. Etienne (such a contrast in its Gothic habiliments to the toga-like dress of its neighbour) which is really the *clou* of his lithograph. Many figures are to be seen wandering about, perhaps all going to a service in the church whose oil-lamp seems to beckon them and to light up in its feeble way what is left unlighted by the moon.

I have not been able to find any signature on the plate. Its darkness would have made it, in any case, difficult to trace one.

THIS picture has a special interest in that it is the only one of the lithographs forming the present volume of which the original in a completed form is known to exist. The water-colour from which it was taken is among the collection of Boys's works in that medium, now in the Victoria and Albert Museum. There is another point of interest about the lithograph, for it is one of the many views of Paris which Boys executed during his first residence in the French capital, most of those included in the *Picturesque Architecture* being produced at a later period. Although the work is only signed T. Boys without any mention of the year in which its original was produced, that original bears the date 1829, and thus preceded the majority of the pictures in this volume by some ten years.

The title of the water-colour is "A View near the Pont Royal, Paris" (its size being $13\frac{3}{8} \times 10\frac{3}{8}$ inches), but in lithographic form it was more properly called by the title which is that of the chief feature in the composition—*i.e.*, the Pavillon de Flore. As a matter of fact, the Pont Royal, though near enough, is not actually in the picture at all, being, of course, on the left hand, at the end of the parapet, against which the two men (an excellent and very natural group) are leaning. Below this parapet runs the river, and in the distance, broken by the vehicles evidently just having come over the Pont Royal, is the Place de la Concorde and the more distant trees of the Champs Elysées. Today there is a bridge nearer to the spectator than the Pont Royal, namely, the Pont du Carrousel, which, however, did not come into existence till 1834 (it was restored in 1907), just five years after Boys had executed his water-colour drawing. As the title of that drawing specifies the Pont Royal, I may note that that bridge was constructed by François Romain after Mansart's plans in 1685-89 to replace the former one, known variously as the Pont Rouge, Pont des Tuileries, and Pont Barbier, which had been destroyed during the former year. The first attempt to assassinate Louis Philippe took place on this bridge in 1831, just ten years before it was restored.

Turning to the most prominent object in the picture before us, we have a beautiful and, as was to be expected from Boys, an extraordinarily faithful rendering of that south-west corner of the Tuileries known as the Pavillon de Flore.

Before the destruction of the Tuileries by the Commune on May 22, 1871, the palace extended north and south from the Pavillon de Marsan, abutting on the Rue de Rivoli, to the Pavillon de Flore, of whose return frontage facing the river we have here the picture. It was then linked up with the Louvre, and the pink Arc de Carrousel, which is so prominent an object here, was hidden in the vast quadrangle. Hidden there, too, were all sorts of old houses, some of them very dilapidated, many covered by *affiches* of all kinds, as may be seen by a photograph taken from the terrace of the Tuileries about the year 1847. It was part of the vast improvement to Paris, initiated by Napoleon III., with Haussmann as his architectural chief of the staff, that was responsible for linking up the Louvre on the east with the Tuileries (so called, of course, because the

21. *Pavillon de Flore, Tuileries, Paris*

original palace was erected on a spot previously occupied by tin kilns) on the west.

The loss of that splendid façade looking over the gardens which had sprung into being under the wand of the great Lenôtre cannot but be regretted; and yet the vastness of the successive quadrangles thus exposed, with Gambetta flamboyant as ever in stone, in their midst, to some extent reconciles us for the loss. Among landmarks once occupying this *enceinte*, by the way, was the Hotel de Longueville, of the ruins of which an interesting lithograph is extant, as well as other once noble houses gradually fallen from their high estate and become ruinous.

Boys's picture, however, has nothing, save propinquity, to do with these lost features of old Paris. But it was executed while yet Charles X. was on the throne, and gives us a vivid little reminder of the dress and equipages of that period. Incidentally, too, it shows us the means then in vogue of lighting the streets (a picture by Canella, in the Musée Carnavalet, of the Place de la Concorde in the same year perpetuates one of these hanging lamps still more clearly), and gives point to the once terrible cry " à la lanterne."

Without entering into a long account of the construction of the Louvre and the Tuileries, which is here unnecessary, for most people know where to find such data, I may at least mention two points of interest in the picture before us. One is that the lightning conductors shown on the roof of the Louvre were the first, or almost the first, to be erected in Paris; while it was before the gateway, between the two lamps, that Alibaud took his stand when he tried to assassinate Louis Philippe by shooting at him on June 25, 1836, for which he was guillotined at Paris in the following July. As we have seen, an earlier attempt to kill the Patriot King occurred by a coincidence within a stone's-throw of this spot.

IT is apt to be forgotten that the Rue de Rivoli, whose monotonous but convenient arcades and rather meretricious shops, which tourists, however, seem to find so attractive, give its western end an air of modernity and Napoleonic uniformity, becomes further east far less sophisticated and is intersected by all sorts of interesting little byways whose names, if nothing else, recall the Paris of the past. Such an exiguous thoroughfare is the Rue des Bourdonnais which serpentines from the main thoroughfare to the Quai de la Mégisserie, close to the Pont Neuf, on the one hand, and links up the Rue de Rivoli with the Rue St. Honoré on the other. The street was, in the thirteenth century, known as the Rue Adam Bourdon, from the owner of property in it, a name which in course of years became converted into its present one. Its lower portion had at various times other names applied to it, but these do not concern us as it is in the section north of the Rue de Rivoli that the Hotel de Trémouille, of which Boys here gives us a picture, stood. This mansion occupied the site of No. 31 in the street ; and it was lucky that Boys made his sketch of the beautiful fragment, for only a few years later, in 1842, it was demolished and a new building erected on its site. Even as it is we see that the exquisitely decorated tower, sole relic of a once great private palace, is impinged upon on both sides by relatively modern structures. Happily this, although removed, has not actually been destroyed, being preserved in the École des Beaux Arts, just as the front of Sir Paul Pindar's house is safely in harbour at the Victoria and Albert Museum.

When the Hotel de la Trémouille was erected is unknown, but the Duc d'Orleans, father of King John of France, is recorded as inhabiting it in 1363. Twelve years later the Duke sold the mansion, then known as the Hotel des Carnaulx, to Guy de la Trémouille. Later, in 1409, it is found being inhabited by the Bishop of Liège, known as Jean sans Pitié, who occupied it when staying in Paris. During the reign of Charles VI. it became English property for a time, after Henry V. had won the Battle of Agincourt. Then in 1438 a certain Chevalier de la Vodrière is found in possession of the place, which, however, two years later reverted to the Trémouille family, one of whose members, Louis de la Trémouille, reconstructed it in 1489. Ten years later gorgeous fêtes in connection with the celebration of the marriage of Louis XII. and Anne of Brittany were held here. But in the following year the hotel passed into the hands of the treasurer, Pierre le Gendre. To close the list of its successive owners, we know that from 1600 to 1675 it appertained to the family of Le Bellièvre, during which time President Molé occupied it, and then to the Chancellor Dubourg ; while in 1771 the famous physiologist and chemist, Fourcroy, was living here, and later still it descended to the use of some old Jew clothes-men !

Nearly all the houses in this part of the Rue des Bourdonnais are curious and old, but none of them possessed such an apostolic succession of notable occupants as did this one, of which Boys (who signs it humorously " Remise à Louer, s'addresser à T. Boys ") has left us this charming and spirited memorial.

22. *Hotel de la Trémouille, Paris*   22. *Rue Vieille du Temple, Paris*

THAT part of Paris known as the Marais is full of interesting memories and not a few remains of the beautiful architecture of a past day. Here the Middle Ages and the age of Honoré de Balzac seem to link hands, and from the wonderful Hotel de Strasbourg, in the Rue Vieille du Temple, we pass to a house where Corneille's " Cid " was first represented, only to be seduced away by the sign on another of that " Chat qui pélote " which the author of the *Comédie Humaine* borrowed as the title of one of the works forming that tremendous literary monument. There is hardly a street in the Marais which is not full of history : the Rue des Francs Bourgeois, once the principal high street in Paris ; the Rue des Blancs Manteaux, recalling by its name the religious fraternity whose dwelling was here ; the Rue du Roi de Sicile, and a hundred others, the names of nearly all of which are redolent of the picturesque days of the Middle Ages, when the Sieur de Maletot, of our own romancer, lived, and the Villon of fact and legend wandered about the darkened streets and sang of love and villainy.

Of all these streets none are fuller of romance and historic association than the Rue Vieille du Temple, although today so much of it has become hidden beneath a layer of modernity and not a little dirt. Here and there, however, you may catch a glimpse, as it were, of the past, and the most notable of such relics happily remains in the little Tour Barbette, of which Boys gives us his fascinating picture.

This precious little relic juts out into the street at its junction with the Rue Barbette, which links up the Rue Vieille du Temple with the Rue Elzévir. This *tourelle* was erected towards the close of the fifteenth century by Jean de la Balue, the second husband of the widow of Jean Herouët, secretary to Louis II. of Orleans. During the eighteenth century it was in the possession of the family of Tillet de Villarceaux, who held it from 1740 to 1748. Sometimes it is found described as the Tourelle Herouët, sometimes, and more often, as the Tour Barbette ; the latter name having been given it from the neighbouring Courtille Barbette (from which the street is, of course, also named) whose gardens were famous so far back as the thirteenth century, but the history of whose *logis* is far too long and complicated even to be glanced at here.

The *tourelle* is now numbered 54, but apparently in Boys's day it was 68— at least, according to one of the many signs and inscriptions which then hid so much of the beauty of the little relic. The two great boards which wellnigh obliterate it tell us that at No. 24, Rue des Francs Bourgeois was a depot for seltzer water ; and that " Madame Pinard prend pensionnaires," with a representation of the lady herself. The little wine-shop might be that of the Defarges, in *A Tale of Two Cities*. The whole links up the fifteenth and eighteenth centuries with the century of Balzac and Boys, and forms a companion picture to the latter's water-colour of the " House of Admiral Coligny," which possessed a very similar *tourelle*, now in the Reinaecker Collection. By the way, the red-brick house in the background of the picture before us is one of those remaining from the time of Henri Quatre, and is similar to those in the Place des Vosges and the Place Dauphine.

THERE is, perhaps, no more notable building in Paris than the Institut, the headquarters of the French Academy founded by Cardinal Richelieu ; the magnet which has attracted so many great men, and has been responsible for not a few mean actions ; the home of the Immortal Forty, to which Molière and Balzac never belonged, and which aroused the scorn and satire of Alphonse Daudet in *L'Immortel.* That famous dome has been the lodestar of French literature for many generations, and thus it is that, apart from its marked architectural dominance on the left bank of the Seine, its moral effect may be said to be spread throughout the length and breadth of Paris, and, indeed, to have penetrated to some extent into all parts of the habitable and educated globe. Like our own artistic Royal Academy, many are found scoffing at the Institut ; but also, as in the case of Burlington House, it forms the secret goal even of those who affect to despise it. The fact is, neither of these institutions can, by the greatest stretch of the imagination, be regarded as negligible ; and their stone headquarters have taken on something of their mesmeric effect, for they represent the highest pinnacle to which their candidates can reach—in one the spirit of Reynolds, in the other that of Richelieu seems always to dwell.

Boys, therefore, naturally selected this building as one of the characteristic features of Paris, but he, no doubt, did so rather from a decorative than an ethical point of view—rather, that is, as an architectural " subject " than as an emblem of world-wide literary influence.

The buildings of the Institut occupy the site of the Hotel de Nèsle and part of the ground known as the Pré-aux-Clercs, the reading room being said to stand exactly where the romantic and legendary Tour de Nèsle once rose. The structure was built in fulfilment of Mazarin's testamentary instructions, accord-ing to plans drawn out by Louis Levau in 1663, and was completed by Lambert and D'Orbay. It was at first popularly called the College des Quatre Nations, because its primary object had been the reception of sixty young scholars from the annexed provinces of Alsace, Pignerol, Flandre, and Roussillon. In 1791 its name was changed to the Collège de l'Unité, but the whole thing was suppressed in 1793, and a portion of its buildings was for a time converted into a debtor's prison ; while a central school and a School of Fine Arts, founded in 1801, were lodged in other parts. In 1806, however, the place was allocated to the use of the Institut, and the architect, Vaudoyer, was commissioned to recon-struct the building for this purpose, the chapel which had once contained Mazarin's tomb—the work of the famous Coysevox—becoming the hall destined for the public reception of elected members.

The actual foundation of this Institution, as it exists today, dates from 1795, but the Academie Française, of which it is the offspring, so to say, was due to the literary interests of Richelieu, and had its origin as far back as 1635.

As a French writer has succinctly put it, " C'est une de ces impérissables

23. *La Chapelle de l'Institut, Paris*

institutions que les railleries qu'il à toujours été de mode de lui décacher n'ont pu entamer encore."

It is characteristic of Boys's eye for an effective *coup d'œil* that he should have selected an angle from which to make his drawing of the Institut. Probably from no other standpoint could its impressiveness be so well indicated as it is from the east. A parallel to this method of depicting a building more or less in perspective is to be found in the artist's picture of St. James's Palace in his *Original Views of London*, where, in contradistinction to most artists who have treated that well-worn subject, he shows it to us from the west side, and thus gives to what has become rather hackneyed, beautiful as it essentially is, a novelty and freshness of treatment all his own.

In the present case the architectural features of the well-known Paris landmark are admirably reproduced, and as it is evening the glow of the setting sun lights up the stonework very effectively. Movement is given to the composition by the women drawing water which spouts from the mouths of the two recumbent lions, designed, by the way, in 1809 by Creusot, who copied them more or less faithfully from those on the Moses Fountain at Rome ; while these figures are linked up by the others in the centre of the picture.

In Boys's day the Place de l'Institut, as we know it, the semi-circular court in front, that is to say, to which the Pont des Arts gives access from the right bank of the river, was merely an unornamented open space. It was not formed, indeed, till 1862, although the bridge itself had been constructed in 1804, and restored in 1854. Until 1849, those passing across this bridge had to pay a toll of a halfpenny. In 1880, the fountain shown in the picture was replaced by a rather indifferent and insignificant statue representing the Republic, designed by the sculptor Soitoux.

The lithograph is signed by Boys, and is dated 1838.

THOSE who would see the exterior of Notre Dame to the best advantage should not fail to visit the tiny little Norman Church of St. Julien-le-Pauvre, which lies hidden away rather to the east of St. Sévérin, and which is so little generally known that I have met Parisians who are unacquainted with it, for from its little garden, into which the civil custodian is always ready to admit visitors, one obtains a complete vista of the whole southern side of the cathedral, from its two famous west towers to those flying buttresses at the east end which are among its most attractive architectural features. Another fine point of vantage for considering the general beauty of the structure is to view it from the east in order to be reminded of Méryon's superb etching of it from this standpoint. And there is also a third possible *coup d'œil*, somewhere between the two, which is hardly less satisfying, and is that where Boys took his stand when he produced the accompanying picture.

Here we are with the artist on what is known as the Quai St. Bernard, but which in ancient days was called the Vieux-Chemin-d'Ivry. This quay owes its name to the Porte St. Bernard which used to stand where the Pont Sully joins the south bank of the Seine ; and the Rue des Fossés St. Bernard which runs into it from the south further perpetuates the name of the French monk of Cluny who lived in the twelfth century and who wrote the Latin poem known as " De Contemptu Mundi."

Apart from the famous cathedral itself, what will probably be most striking to anyone examining this exquisite picture is the long row of bathing and washing sheds which flank the wall of the Isle de la Cité on which Notre Dame is situated. These bathing-places have, indeed, an ancestry dating from the days of Louis XIV., when they were celebrated for their fair and frail clientèle, people going specially to see the beautiful demi-mondaines of the period disporting themselves in the water.

The dilapidated houses on the left, from the windows of which so much washing is hanging, screen the Church of St. Julien from us, and although, today, rebuilding has taken place here, there still remain gaps and half-demolished structures, which give to Boys's view, old as it now is, a certain air of familiarity. The little bridge we see is the Pont au Double, which was constructed in 1634, but which in recent times (1881) has been rebuilt.

This Pont au Double has an interesting history. Originally it was not meant as a passage-way at all. The fact is the neighbouring Hotel Dieu had at the beginning of the seventeenth century become overcrowded, and it sought permission to construct an additional ward* on a structure built across the river from the south bank to the Isle de la Cité. This suggestion was at first strongly opposed, but eventually, in 1626 to be precise, it materialized, the architect Gamard executing the plans. When the inhabitants of the neighbourhood on the south side of the river realized that the bridge was to be constructed, they offered to contribute to its cost on the condition that they should be

* This building is shown in a view of Notre Dame from the east, executed by J. C. Nattes.

24. *Notre Dame from the Quai St. Bernard, Paris*

allowed to use it, and the authorities of the Hotel Dieu, nothing loth, made a kind of *double* turnstile, one side for foot-passengers and the other for horsemen. In course of time many people tried to cross without payment, especially those who were armed and who were thus able to support more or less effectively their claim to a free passage. The Royal Authority was invoked on behalf of the Hotel Dieu, and all sorts of drastic pains and penalties were enforced, even so far as the right to throw recalcitrants into the Seine ! The bridge was completed in 1632, and soon after the Hotel Dieu began the erection of a great building, part of which stood on the first arch of the bridge on the Isle de la Cité side. This structure, which was one of great size, surmounted by an enormous roof, was called St. Charles, and was also designed by Gamard. I may add that in 1651 another bridge, called Pont de l'Hotel Dieu, was built connecting the other end of the new edifice with the mainland. It was not till 1789 that the tolls on the Pont au Double were done away with.

Just beyond is the Petit Pont, which occupies the spot where in Roman days two bridges existed. Formerly it was encumbered with mills and wooden houses, and although reconstructed in stone as far back as 1185, was continually being destroyed by fire, no fewer than eleven conflagrations having taken place on it down to the year 1718, when it was at last rebuilt without houses on it. The bridge Boys knew and has here perpetuated was this last, for it was not till 1853 that the present structure replaced it.

I know few pictures which give such a striking picture of the apposition of the squalid and dilapidated to the architectural splendour of Paris as does this one. The ruinous dwellings, the very casks covered by tarpaulin in the foreground, the evidences of poverty in the houses, and the general air of ruin on the south bank, throw into relief in a specially vivid way the beautiful outlines of Notre Dame, and help to form a scene very characteristic of the French capital during the earlier half of the last century.

Boys's signature will be found on the lithograph, but without a date.

WE know from one of his letters that Lord Macaulay was rather disappointed with Chartres Cathedral. But he suffered from the overlaudation of those who knew it, and who had described it to him as one of the most magnificent in Europe. "Now," he writes, "I have seen finer Gothic churches in England, France, and Belgium. It wants vastness; and its admirers make the matter worse by proving to you that it is a great deal larger than it looks, and by assuring you that the proportions are so exquisite as to produce the effect of littleness," and he proceeds to show the fallacy of what he calls this cant—*i.e.*, that a building should be made to look smaller than it actually is, instead of larger. But even Macaulay owns that Chartres is a fine church; and if one wanted support for this, one could hardly find a better than the exquisite character of this Porch of which Boys has left such a remarkable picture. Indeed, in spite of the historian's faint praise, Chartres Cathedral is recognized as one of the great sacred edifices of the world; one of those structures dating from the twelfth and thirteenth centuries the solidity and grace of which go hand in hand and seem to prove that really noble architecture possesses the dual quality of masculine strength and feminine beauty and grace.

The oldest part of the building is the west end with its three wonderful porches, in which the audacity and charm of the sculpture is only surpassed by that on the north and south, which is still more elaborately decorated. It is the latter of these porches which is the subject of Boys's picture; and those who are acquainted with the great Gothic cathedral—in which, by the way, Henri Quatre was crowned in 1594—will realize how truthful is his rendering of " the frozen music" produced by the artificers of six hundred and more years ago. The artist has taken up a position nearly under the great portal, in order to emphasize the remarkable character of the carved stonework, representing the Last Judgment, which adorns it. The consequence is that the figures he introduces into his picture, and which here, as elsewhere, are so important as affording the idea of relative size to the building delineated, are considerably larger than is usual with him. This fact helps to give us rather the idea of one of David Roberts's careful and graphic studies than of the more precise work of his contemporary. Indeed, had the picture not been signed " T. Boys, 1839," I should have been inclined to attribute it to Roberts, who, according to some statements, did actually supply one of the subjects in the present volume.

For those who do not know Chartres Cathedral I may remark that, of its specially notable features, the spire and south tower are generally regarded as among the finest, if not actually the finest, of their particular type. The interior, while not so ornate as the outside, is instinct with a quiet dignity not less impressive. Among other notable characteristics are the amazing windows, no fewer than one hundred of which possess the original glass set in them during the thirteenth century ! Another remarkable feature of the interior is the series of sculptured figures representing the life of Christ and the Virgin Mary, on the

25. *South Porch of Chartres Cathedral*

choir-screen, the accompanying tracery of which is a marvel of carving in the Flamboyant style.

In Boys's picture, which represents thus only one of the many beauties of this incomparable pile, one should not omit to notice the interesting building on the opposite side of the space before the cathedral, with its attractive pillared upper part and its ecclesiastical air coinciding with its environment so deftly, and looking like a little piece of monasticism (as, indeed, it no doubt is) incorporated in the dwellings of a later day. The building seen through the Porch, which is the entrance to the south transept of the cathedral, was, in the artist's day, being used as a hospital.

Apart from the cathedral, which is, by common consent, one of the most remarkable that even France, with all her wealth in this direction, has to show, Chartres contains a mass of entrancing architectural objects, which are far better known now than they were in Boys's time. Its old houses, with their yellow and white and bluish-grey façades, which are so effective when the sun lights them up, are among its attractive features; its outstanding landmarks, such as the famous Escalier de la Reine Berthe, the Church of St. Aignan, and so forth, being, however, the chief objectives of the visitor. But, after all, the cathedral is so dominating, such a brilliant architectural jewel, that it casts into the shade gems of lesser lustre. I never think of that wonderful structure without calling to mind the etching by Mr. George Marples, entitled "The Jackdaws of Chartres." For there we are wafted to the top of one of the towers, and look down on the projecting gargoyles round which the birds are whirling, with the city of old roofs laid out like a map beneath us. "The Jackdaws of Chartres" forms, indeed, a companion picture to Méryon's famous "Stryge," in which we have a not dis similar view of Paris from the towers of Notre Dame.

HAVING given us a view of the south porch of Chartres Cathedral, Boys, instead of further expatiating pictorially on other features of this amazing pile, has gone elsewhere in the city to find something architecturally distinctive in another style, and he has, therefore, selected for this purpose the little Church of St. André, of which he here represents the west front. As is known, the River Eure runs through the city in various branches, one of which skirts the Rue du Massacre, and it is between these two boundaries and the Rue St. André that the ancient edifice depicted by the artist stands.

Chartres, besides its dominating cathedral and the small Church of St. André, possesses at least two other sacred edifices which are worth examination. One of these is St. Aignan, standing in its little precincts between the Rue St. Pierre and the Rue des Grenets. It is a composite structure, exhibiting examples of the thirteenth, sixteenth, and seventeenth centuries, the last rather debased period being, as is not unusual with buildings that have been added to from time to time, the most prominent. The other church is that of St. Pierre, which is more noticeable, for it is the outcome of the eleventh and thirteenth centuries, and therefore its architecture is better worth studying. But besides this, it possesses an important and attractive feature within, in the form of twelve remarkable Limoges enamels, the work of Bernard Limousin (1505-77), the greatest of all the workers in this medium. These precious objects came from the famous Chateau d'Anet, built for Diana of Poitiers by Henri II., and designed by his architect, Philibert Delorme. That place is today but a ruin, much of it being destroyed during the French Revolution, when the tomb of its mistress in the adjoining chapel was rifled and her monument pulled down, although happily some sculpture by the great Jean Goujon remains. But this has carried us far away from Chartres and its architectural treasures, and I return to the city in order to say something about its history and the special object of Boys's lithographic perpetuation.

With regard, then, to the city itself, it may not be generally known, as the phrase goes, that it is one of the most ancient in France. So old, indeed, is it that it is credibly said to have been founded by the tribe of the Carnutes, with whom, by the way, Cæsar fought in 52-51 B.C. It was later destined to become the seat of what was known as the College of Druids, whose members congregated in this neighbourhood as well as round Dreux close by. In course of time the city became the capital of the province of Beauce, and later gave its name to those powerful nobles, the Counts of Chartres, who had so much to do with the original formation of the French monarchy. During the wars of religion and those whose object was rather personal aggrandizement than religious sentiment, Chartres was frequently the centre of conflict, and Normans and Burgundians and so forth besieged it with more or less success during the years when their rivalry made cities and towns the objective, in some cases of mere cupidity, in others of a larger-minded policy.

26. *St. André, Chartres*

But in spite of these turbulent happenings no event of special importance connected with Chartres emerges till 1594, on February 27 of which year Henri Quatre was here crowned king with great decorative ceremonial. In 1870 the Germans made themselves masters of the place, which was one of strategic importance in the operations during the Franco-Prussian War. Chartres, with its old houses, its narrow and often tortuous streets, and an air of mediævalism which, in spite of much modernity, still clings to it, seems a place made for the activities of the artist and the dreams of the poet. Russell Lowell may be said to have fulfilled the latter expectations in his poem entitled " The Cathedral," while Boys has given us, as examples of the former, these two graphic illustrations of the Cathedral and of this little church of St. André.

In this aspect of the latter edifice there may be discerned three successive architectural styles, but its chief characteristic is as a beautiful specimen of the period in which it was begun, with its Norman doorway, the pillar capitals of which exhibit an extraordinary delicacy of treatment. Above this entrance is the curious " Marygold " window, specially noticeable on account of its singularity and intrinsic beauty. In the interior are some interesting frescoes dating from the twelfth century, while in a side-chapel is a feature which is rarely to be found in French churches, namely a roof of Fan Tracery very beautiful and attractive in design.

Boys has, as usual, introduced the human element into his picture, in the shape of a group of two women and a donkey, while his initials and date—T.B., 1839—will be observed on the packet borne on the trolley to which a horse is attached.

Index

Index